Y0-CKN-984

The Triumph of Age

The Triumph of Age

*How to feel young
and happy in retirement*

by
DR. DOROTHY C. FINKELHOR

FOLLETT PUBLISHING COMPANY
CHICAGO

Designed by Karen Yops.
Edited by Susan David.

Copyright © 1979 by Dorothy C. Finkelhor.
All rights reserved. No portion of this book may be used or reproduced in any manner whatsoever without written permission from the publisher except in the case of brief quotations embodied in critical reviews and articles. Manufactured in the United States of America.

Library of Congress Cataloging in Publication Data

Finkelhor, Dorothy C.   1902–
  The triumph of age.

  Bibliography: p.
  1. Retirement—United States. I. Title.
HQ1062.F56   301.43′5   78–10162
ISBN 0-695-81136-3

To my husband, with whom
I tested the guidelines
of this book and made
our retirement years the
best years of our lives.

Other Books by
Dr. Dorothy C. Finkelhor

THE LIBERATED GRANDMOTHER
HOW TO MAKE YOUR EMOTIONS
WORK FOR YOU

Contents

1 Your Key to Feeling Young and Happy in Retirement   11

2 How to Get Rid of Middle-aged Responsibilities   22

3 How to Know and Like Yourself in Retirement   42

4 How to Make Decisions That Solve Retirement Problems   57

5 How to Get What You Want from Yourself and Other People   67

6 How to Get What You Want from Life   85

7 How to Communicate with Younger People   105

8 How to Make Your Marriage Better Than Before   121

9 How to Deal with Your Fear of Death   140

10 How to Turn Loneliness into Happiness   151

11	Sex After Sixty-five	174
12	Emotional Blackmail Against Older People	189
13	The Shock of Mandatory Retirement	202
14	The Retirement Community—Paradise or Purgatory?	218
15	How to Gain Respect in an Ageist Community	232
16	How to Predict Your Own Future	248
	Suggested Readings	261

The Triumph of Age

1

Your Key to Feeling Young and Happy in Retirement

This retired couple is in trouble. They spat continually over little things. There's tension between them and their married children. Money isn't a pressing problem, but they fuss and fret about it. They don't seem to get along with anybody. When they're not squabbling or complaining, they sit and mope and worry about tomorrow. They're in their sixties, but they feel old.

Meanwhile, the retired couple next door is happy and productive, with warm family relationships, many friends, no worries to speak of, and confidence in themselves and their future. They're in their seventies, but they feel young.

What makes one retired couple feel young and happy while another feels old and troubled?

Let's look in on an unhappy couple and a happy couple facing the same retirement situation. The husband has just retired; the wife has not been working. It's a familiar story—the husband hangs around the house all day, and the wife is irritated by it.

THE UNHAPPY COUPLE

The wife does nothing about her aggravation. She lets it build up slowly inside her until it explodes into nagging and quarreling. She shrieks at him, "You're always underfoot."

He can't understand her resentment. He shouts back, "I'm your husband. This is my home. I have a perfect right to be here."

What do they blame their brawls on? "We're getting old." They feel old. And look it, too. There's nothing like unhappiness to speed up the aging clock.

Everyone ages. But getting older in years is not the reason for the unhappiness of these two. This is: They did nothing to solve the retirement problem they faced as they got older. They gave their emotions free rein to work *against* them. That's a sign of emotional immaturity.

THE HAPPY COUPLE

The wife, who's had the house to herself for so long, suddenly finds a man around all day long. "Of course, I feel irritated. Who wouldn't?" She realizes she has a problem. But instead of letting it get her down, she resolves to do something about it. And she does. She plans activities for herself outside the house. And, more important, she tries to get her husband interested in getting out and doing things on his own, too.

His first reaction? "I resent being kicked out of my own home." Now it's his turn to realize he has a problem. He can let it eat at him, but he doesn't. Like his wife, he resolves to do something about it. And he does. For starters, he decides to follow in Gerald Ford's footsteps. When

President Ford became ex-President Ford, he promised Betty he'd never come home for lunch. This understanding husband can do no less.

Then, as his wife suggested, he gets himself involved in a number of out-of-the-house projects. That makes his day more interesting and him more interesting when he comes home. What's more, when he is in the house, he shares the housework. "If you had told me a year ago," he admits, "that I'd be loading the dishwasher and doing the laundry, I'd have said you had to be out of your mind. But I don't feel like an extra wheel anymore. I feel I'm needed."

What's his wife's reaction? "Welcome aboard!"

What do they credit for their happiness? "We refused to feel old." These two people, married for nearly forty years, feel as if they're playing house together. "It's like turning back the clock to our early marriage days," the wife beams. "We feel full of life again." And they look it. There's no cosmetic that beats happiness.

How did they refuse to feel old? They didn't let their retirement-marriage problem age them. She took her irritation and converted it into positive acts. He did the same with his resentment. They solved their retirement problem by making their emotions work *for* them. That's a sign of emotional maturity.

There are few retired couples as bleakly unhappy and few as blissfully happy as the couples in these dramatizations. On a scale of 0 to 10, most happy retired couples would score about 8, and most unhappy ones about 3. But no matter what their ratings on the happiness meter, one thing is certain. The difference between a happy retired couple and an unhappy one is just this: The happy couple is emotionally mature for retirement; the unhappy couple is not.

Happiness makes you feel young. Unhappiness makes you feel old. Your key to feeling young and happy in retirement is *emotional maturity*.

You were always an emotionally mature person. Will you be emotionally mature in retirement?

Not necessarily. Here's why.

Each stage of life has its own problems. When you can put your emotions to work for you to lick those problems, you're emotionally mature for your stage of life. There's an emotional maturity appropriate for adolescence, another for young adulthood, another for middle age—and there's a specific emotional maturity necessary for retirement. (A person taking early retirement also needs to develop an emotional maturity appropriate for his or her changing life-style.)

As you progress from middle age to "young old-age" (as opposed to "old old-age"), you must acquire a new kind of emotional maturity. As you grow older, you must continue to grow emotionally. If you don't, no matter how emotionally mature you were, you won't be emotionally mature for retirement.

You're emotionally mature for middle age (but not for retirement). What happens when you try to lick your retirement problems?

Retirement has its own special problems—none of which you've ever encountered before. Unless you're emotionally mature *for retirement*, the pleasant stroll through your "golden" years that you had anticipated could turn out to be a scramble blindfolded through a minefield.

Remember the problems typical of the former stages of your life—Saturday nights in adolescence; choosing and pursuing a direction in young adulthood; and kids, cars, and careers in middle age. And just think what would happen if an adolescent, no matter how able to handle the problems of that particular age, tried to solve the problems of his or her parents. Sheer disaster!

The same thing will happen when an emotionally mature middle-ager tries to solve your retirement problems. You could be that emotionally mature middle-ager if you refuse to grow emotionally as you grow older chronologically. Remain stuck in emotional middle age and you'll never be able to solve your retirement problems.

Just how does solving your retirement problems make you feel vital and happy?

In two ways.

BY ABOLISHING PROBLEM-RELATED STRESS

Stress not only makes you feel old but also actually ages you. Here's how.

Stress drains you of your emotional energy. Emotional energy is your driving force, the power that makes you go. You have just so much of it. When stress steals it from you, there's none left with which to handle your everyday problems. You feel listless and spent. Everything's too much for you.

Convince yourself by looking in once again on that unhappy couple—the wife shrieking, the husband shouting back. They're throwing their emotional energy away.

Now look at them when the quarrel is over. They have no emotional energy left. They feel all washed out. The wife complains, "I don't think I could even get up and get a glass of water."

If that's how you react to small problems, imagine how utterly helpless you'll be in the face of the great problems you're bound to meet in retirement—like the strains that threaten to tear your marriage apart, loneliness, and death. You'll feel incapable, frustrated, and defeated.

You'll feel you have no life left in you. And *that's* feeling old.

Stress assaults you physically and mentally. Your legs feels like lead. You're a mess of aches and pains. You're always tired. "When I get up in the morning," a despondent retired businessman moaned, "I don't know where I'll get the strength to get through the day."

Your mind refuses to function no matter how much coffee you drink. Your thoughts won't jell. You worry yourself sick about your failing memory. "I feel I've just had it," this retired businessman said. "I just want to go someplace and have somebody take care of me."

You feel you're falling apart (and you *are*). And *that's* feeling old.

BY BRINGING OUT POSITIVE RATHER THAN NEGATIVE EMOTIONS ABOUT YOURSELF

When you feel good about yourself, you feel happy. And happiness, according to medical researchers specializing in the problems of aging, has just the opposite effect that stress has on your emotional energy and your health. Here's what happens.

When you can't solve your retirement problems, you feel depressed, frustrated, angry, afraid, resentful, and so on. There are thirty negative emotions you're likely to feel in retirement (see chapter 3), and failure to solve your retirement problems will bring out each emotion at one time or another.

But when you're emotionally mature for retirement, you can meet these problems with the ability to beat them. What do you feel when you win? Delight, satisfaction, pleasure, and so on. For each of the thirty negative emotions that get you down in retirement, there are thirty positive emotions that buoy you up.

You feel up to doing almost anything. Your body's physical decline actually slows down. Often, it seems to stop. The happy expression on your face takes years off your age. Your mind is as sharp as you always knew it could be. You welcome challenges; you find zest in everything; you're full of life and rarin' to go. And *that's* feeling young—at any age.

You don't have to be retired to feel old. I've interviewed men and women who felt old at fifty, at forty, even at thirty. They were emotionally immature people who couldn't solve the problems of their stage of life and succumbed to stress.

On the other hand, I know an eighty-four-year-old woman who runs a stenographic service, gives cooking lessons, and writes children's books. She doesn't look a day over seventy, and I've never seen her when she wasn't doing something or dreaming up something. "Where does she get all her energy?" people wonder. She gets it from her emotional maturity, which enables her to lick the problems of old age. She could never be the victim of problem-induced stress.

"When am I supposed to start feeling old?" this happy woman asks me.

"Never!" I answer.

You could have the same answer about yourself—when you are emotionally mature for retirement.

How can you tell whether you're emotionally mature for retirement?

The battery of instruments in your doctor's lab will tell you whether you're physically fit *for your age*. This book will help you measure whether you're emotionally mature *for your age.*

I've developed a quiz that measures your emotional quotient, or EQ, for *your* age—the retirement age. The quiz is so simple you can breeze through it in two or three minutes. Take it and find out for yourself whether you are emotionally mature for retirement. (And also find out some things about yourself you may never have known before.)

WHAT'S YOUR RETIREMENT EQ (EMOTIONAL QUOTIENT)?*

On a separate sheet of paper, answer the following questions yes or no. Your answers represent the emotions you feel when you encounter fifteen specific retirement situations. Each question typifies a key problem area of retirement. Within each area, you're likely to encounter dozens of problems. Your answers will tell you whether you have the ability to put your emotions to work for you to solve the problems that arise. When you can do that, you're emotionally mature for retirement.

Following the quiz you'll find instructions for scoring your answers.

Important: Write down your answers with a pen. You'll want a permanent record in order to use every answer—right ones and wrong ones—to help you reach emotional maturity for retirement. (I'll tell you how in chapter 3.) So when you take this test,

---

* This quiz first appeared in *Modern Maturity,* June–July 1978.

Your Key to Feeling Young and Happy in Retirement 19

don't worry if your answers are right or wrong. Knowing what your answers are is what will pay off.

1. When you say no to your children's requests for money, do you feel guilty?

2. Do you get irritated living with your marriage partner twenty-four hours a day?

3. Do you feel that you must entertain like other retired people who seem to lead a more active social life?

4. Does every little ache and pain make you feel blue?

5. Are you afraid that your mental abilities are slipping?

6. Are you too close-minded to try new ways of improving yourself now that you have the time to do so?

7. Do you feel disrespected by strangers?

8. Do you feel bored when you have time on your hands?

9. Are you excessively worried about the rising cost of living?

10. Do you feel resentful when you're on a special diet?

11. Does thinking about a move to smaller quarters make you angry?

12. Are you frustrated because you don't make money from your hobbies?

13. Do you feel selfish when you refuse to do voluntary work to help others because you don't get paid?

14. Are you envious of retired couples who travel more than you do?

15. Are you very anxious about the possibility of an accident in your home?

Now go over each yes answer and ask yourself; Do I do something constructive about each emotion, or do I let it build up inside of me like a head of steam in a pressure cooker until I blow my top?

For each emotion you do do something constructive about, give yourself 10 points. Add 10 points for each no. Total up your score. That's your retirement EQ.

A retirement EQ of 150 means you're emotionally mature for retirement. (If you don't have living children or a living spouse, your top score will be 130.)

A retirement EQ of less than 150 means you're emotionally immature for retirement. But don't think you're a special case. Most retirees who take this quiz score from 80 to 100. That doesn't mean they're hopeless. It means they're on their way to achieving emotional maturity for their stage of life. With some work, they can reach 150.

And so can you.

You may not be able to do anything about your IQ (intelligence quotient) in retirement, but you *can* boost your EQ—and your EQ is far more important than your IQ when it comes to solving your retirement problems. Reach an EQ of 150 and you should be able to solve *all* of them. When that happens, you'll feel alive and happy.

In the next three chapters, I'll show you four guidelines to send you on your way to achieving emotional maturity for retirement. And in the process, you'll learn how to live a new life of freedom, without the burden of middle-aged emotional hangups; how to get reacquainted with the real "me" who might have been hidden inside you for forty years or more; how to like yourself in retirement, a feat at any age; and how to make the most emotionally satisfying decisions for yourself.

2

How to Get Rid of Middle-aged Responsibilities

There are four guidelines for achieving emotional maturity in retirement. The first is

Get rid of your middle-aged responsibilities.

Responsibilities are emotional bonds. The responsibilities of middle age bind you emotionally to middle age. As long as you hold on to them, you cannot grow emotionally into the next stage of your life; you cannot reach emotional maturity in retirement.

But before you can get rid of your middle-aged responsibilities, you've got to know what they are. How many major responsibilities of middle age can you name? Responsibility to make a living. That's one. Responsibility to bring up the kids. That's two. And at this point, most retirees throw up their hands and say, "That's all."

But is it all? You're in for an eye-opening surprise. Discover for yourself the full range of your middle-aged responsibilities by answering yes or no to the following questions. Important: Think of yourself as middle-aged when you answer.

DISCOVER YOUR MIDDLE-AGED RESPONSIBILITIES
---

1. Do you feel you still must take care of your children—even though it means sacrifices on your part?

2. Do you feel you have to have a job to keep your self-respect? (Money is not the issue here.)

3. Do you feel you have to live up to the lifestyle of your friends and neighbors?

4. Do you feel it's a must to lead a social life approved of by your friends?

5. Do you feel obligated to hang on to your house and car at all costs?

6. Do you feel you're required to take care of your ailing parents yourself?

7. Do you feel it's mandatory to share virtually all your nonwork activities with your marriage partner—even though it means compromise and self-denial?

8. Do you feel a duty to your parents to be the kind of person they taught you to be?

9. Do you feel a compulsion to redo your past failures and successes to make them better?

If you responded like a typical middle-aged American, you answered yes to every question. And every yes means you've assumed a major responsibility. Reviewing the questions from 1 to 9, you discover you have the responsibilities to

1. sacrifice yourself for your children
2. hold a job to keep your self-esteem
3. keep up with the Joneses
4. lead a social life approved of by your friends
5. hold on to your house and car
6. care for your ailing parents yourself
7. live in total togetherness with your marriage partner
8. be the kind of person your parents taught you to be
9. redo your failures as well as your successes to make them better

In middle age, you carry a heavier burden of responsibilities than you realize.

If you're like most middle-agers, you carry this burden with you into retirement. You do this for two reasons. Since you don't want to grow old, you try to slow down the aging clock by clinging to your middle-aged way of life. And you feel that if you drop your responsibilities, you'll be shirking your duty and will therefore become consumed with guilt.

On the surface, these seem like two solid reasons for remaining in emotional middle age. But they don't stand up under analysis.

So far as staying young is concerned, holding on to middle-aged emotional attitudes defeats your purpose. As I pointed out in the preceding chapter, when you try to solve your retirement problems with the attitudes of middle age—even when those attitudes are mature for middle age—you're certain to fail. The resulting stress will age you fast.

So far as shirking your duty is concerned, you don't

have any duty to shirk. Responsibilities necessary for your happiness in middle age are *not* necessary in retirement. In retirement, the responsibilities of your middle age serve no purpose. They don't do you any good, and they can cause you a great deal of harm. Responsibilities that were emotional necessities in middle age are emotional overloads in later years. You may not be able to carry them long without an emotional collapse. Far from feeling guilty when you get rid of them, you should feel a sense of relief.

The way to get rid of your middle-aged responsibilities is to convince yourself that they are no longer needed and that they may very well harm you. Do it for each of your nine middle-aged responsibilities.

HOW TO CONVINCE YOURSELF THAT YOUR MIDDLE-AGED RESPONSIBILITIES ARE USELESS IN RETIREMENT

1. How to convince yourself that in retirement you don't have to sacrifice yourself for your children

As your children were growing up, it was your duty —no matter what the sacrifices—to provide for their well-being and to prepare them to get along in the world. If you're like many people, you continue to cling to this responsibility when your children have reached adulthood. You continue to play the role of "a parent of growing children."

But just stop to consider that your children are grown, and you'll see how empty that role is. You've taught them to stand on their own two feet. They don't need you.

"But my children will always need me," many older fathers and mothers protest. That's just an excuse for refusing to budge from middle age. Ask your adult children point-blank, "Do you really need me the way you used to?"

If you've brought them up to take care of themselves, they'll answer honestly, "No, we don't. We're grateful for everything you did, but we can get along fine now. Don't worry about us. Live your own life."

If they're truly not able to take care of themselves, it could be because you never let them. It's time you cut the silver cord. If you're reluctant to let go, remember that nature will force you to let go when you die, and for an older person that can be sooner than you think. When you're gone, your children will have to grow up with brutal suddenness. Help them grow up now, when you can pick them up if they stumble.

When you continue in retirement to play the role of a parent of growing children, you continue to make sacrifices—from which you can no longer recover. You can't rebuild your depleted savings. But more important, you can never get back the emotional energy you expend on your children's problems. You may not have enough left to solve your own. You put your retirement happiness in jeopardy.

This does not mean you must cut yourself off from your children. You will always be a part of their lives, as they will always be a part of yours. That means you will always have responsibilities to one another. On your part, you'll help them in emergencies or whenever circumstances make it impossible for them to help themselves. You'll be there when they've done everything they can to help themselves but still need you. However, that's not the same as the obligation to sacrifice everything for them on a day-to-day basis.

If the sense of responsibility you felt for your children as they were growing up is scaled at 100, the sense of responsibility you should feel for them in retirement should not exceed 20. That gives you 80 percent more emotional energy to meet problems that are strictly yours.

2. How to convince yourself that in retirement you don't have to hold a job to keep your self-respect

You could have been an individual who liked your job and led a relatively pressure-free life, and your self-respect could have been high. But the point is that a job doesn't necessarily bring you self-respect. The idea that it always does is a myth to cover up the hard-to-live-with fact that many jobs are disagreeable, stress-inducing, or both.

In middle age, you need the myth mentioned above in order to play your role as "a worker." In retirement, your working days are over. There isn't much reason to hold on to the myth. But if you're like many retirees, you'll hold on to it, anyway. You'll continue to feel that without a job you can't have self-respect. And this is what may happen to you.

You may suffer humiliation if you get turned down when looking for a new job. (It's difficult to get a good job at forty, no less at sixty-five or older.) Or maybe you'll take any job you can get. And what will that do to your self-respect? Or perhaps you'll settle for a job substitute, some sort of volunteer work, and try to kid yourself that you're really working. But when week after week goes by without a paycheck, you'll realize you're just playing games—and your self-respect will hit bottom.

When you get rid of your responsibility to have a job in order to keep your self-respect, you gain a new freedom. It's your freedom to work or not to work in retirement. If you can afford it, you can go fishing every day of the year—without a twinge of guilt.

3. How to convince yourself that in retirement you don't have to keep up with the Joneses

Everybody talks about life-style, but few people stop to think about what it is. It's simply the way you spend your money and your time. You can spend it on bowling, beer, and movies. You can spend it on wine, women, and song. You can spend it on trips abroad, college educations for your children, and antiques for your home. But in your middle years, no matter what you spend your money on, you may find yourself spending it to gain status in the eyes of your peer group—your fellow workers, your business associates, and the people in your community.

But in retirement, your peer group usually disintegrates fast. Your fellow workers go their separate ways. Your friends and neighbors move away or pass away. You may decide to relocate and leave them behind. In any case, the pressure is off. You can spend your money any way you like. One retired woman told me, "I can still afford to buy the way I used to. But now I don't have to. And I don't want to."

But if you're like many retirees, you continue to play the role of "the competitive consumer." It has all the drawbacks it had in middle age. You're engaged in a struggle that drains your dollars, your health, and your emotional energy. But you're doing this at a time when you have fewer dollars, when your health is less likely to stand up under the assaults of stress, and when you need all the emotional energy you can muster to meet the new retirement problems you face. The result can be personal bankruptcy, a shattered household, neuroses, and stress-induced diseases.

A clinical psychologist who did a sociological study on some tenants of a posh retirement condominium in Florida concludes that many people who carry their middle-aged consumer competitiveness with them as they age are depressed, psychosomatic, and impotent, and are flocking to doctors.

It's a high price to pay for your sense of responsibility to a middle-aged peer group that is vanishing or has vanished. When you stop keeping up with the Joneses, you start to save the rest of your life.

4. How to convince yourself that in retirement you don't have to lead a social life approved of by your friends

Being together with other human beings, the interchange of thoughts and feelings and the sharing of interests and joys, is one of the richest experiences of our lives—provided you can choose the other human beings you want to spend your time with, and provided you can choose the ways you spend your time with them. In your middle years, you often may not be able to do either.

You have a limited choice of friends. They're usually your fellow workers, your business associates, and the people in your community. Your social life is thrust on you—you're expected to socialize.

Good? Bad? That's a matter of personal preference. Some people like to have their leisure cut out for them, just as they like to have their work cut out for them. Others hate the restrictions put on the relatively few hours of their lives they can call their own. If you fall into the second category described, you'll welcome the realization that in retirement you've passed beyond the reach of your peer group. As I've already pointed out, chances are that most of your peers will soon be out of your life. They won't be able to tell you what to do anymore.

What happens if by some chance your peers stay in your life? What happens, for example, if they all graduate into retirement together and stay together? In that case, you may want to follow the trail of a relocating retiree who told me, "All my friends are moving to the same section of Fort Lauderdale. I'm not going there. I don't want them dictating to me anymore how I'm going to spend my time and who I'm going to spend it with."

But if you enjoyed playing the role of "a social conformist" in middle age, you're likely to want to continue to play it. That may lead you to the retirement communities where the approved pattern of social activity is a continuation of your former social life. But that social activity may become a monotonous routine, and if you're like many retirees, the lack of challenge produces boredom, ineptitude, and a draining of self-confidence. You throw away vast amounts of emotional energy just to go through the motions of having fun. And you pay dearly—in dollars, in separation from your family, and in removal from the excitement and stimulation of the real world outside.

When you drop the responsibility to lead a social life approved of by your friends, you become your own best friend.

5. How to convince yourself that in retirement you don't have to hold on to your house and your car

If you're like most Americans, you don't regard your house and your car as just properties. They're dreams come true. To keep them, you make sacrifices on the same order as those you made for your growing children. To give up your house and car can rank among the most traumatic experiences of your retirement life.

Yet, it's a prospect you're likely to face as property taxes and home-maintenance costs dig a hole in your savings and the price of gas and oil gushes sky-high. There's one way you can face that prospect calmly, even cheerfully. All you have to do is understand that giving up your house and car is ridding yourself of another middle-aged responsibility that has outgrown its usefulness and can be harmful.

What's wrong with retaining a house and a car in retirement if you can? Nothing. If the house suits you. If your car is useful. If the money you spend on upkeep can't be put to better use. But if none of these "ifs" apply, there's a lot wrong. Then you're clinging to your home and your car only because you haven't rid yourself of your middle-aged responsibility to own them. That could lead to obsessive behavior that is self-defeating. Here's a case in point.

A nurse sold her car shortly after retirement because she seldom used it. A few months later, she had to take a trip out of town. She rented a car. "I don't know what happened to me," she recounted, "but when I got behind the wheel and I thought, 'This is not my own car,' I felt I was wronging myself. I *should* have my own car. I went right out and bought myself one."

But it wasn't just any car. To ease the bad feeling caused by believing she *ought* to own a car, she bought a silver Cadillac with red markings—the most expensive car she had ever owned. It virtually wiped out her rainy-day fund. The car spends almost all its time in the garage.

Here's another case.

A retired widower lived alone. He decided that keeping up a large house wasn't a smart thing for him. He sold it and moved to an apartment. His daughters visited him and complained tearfully, "Oh, Dad, you've sold our house." It wasn't their house, but he felt they did have an emotional claim on it. That raked up his middle-aged feeling of responsibility to own a house—after all, he had bought the house for the kids.

"I felt I had let them down," he said. "I couldn't buy another house, so I did the next best thing." There were three rooms in his apartment. He called in a contractor to tear down the walls that separated them. Why did he do it? "To give the impression," he explained, "that it's as roomy as a house." Instead of a cozy apartment, he ended up with a monstrous loft.

Extreme cases? Of course. But they dramatize the pointlessness of holding on to a dead obligation.

Does your home seem like a huge empty edifice now that only you and your spouse rattle around in it? Do you use your car much more sparingly than you did when it took you to work, the children to school, and the family on vacation? One car often wasn't enough. You needed two to carry the load of a growing family. To own a house and one or two cars was as imperative as bringing home a paycheck.

But now your family is gone, and your workdays are over. To hang on to a house too big for you and a car or two for which you have little use is to hang on to not one but two or three white elephants. What was necessary for you then may be too much for you now. It makes no sense to expend emotional energy on the role of "home-and-car owner" when the natural course of events has written that role out of your script. One retired couple learned that lesson the hard way.

Their children were gone, but they stayed behind in the suburban home in which their large family had grown up. "Oh, we knew we were holding on to the past," the wife admitted. "And we knew it was silly not to sell. But we felt some sort of obligation to stay in the old house."

The houses on either side of their home were occupied by couples in their forties. The couple on the right had four children; the couple on the left, three.

"We could see the cars going back and forth," the wife recalled, "the visitors and the delivery men driving up, the comings and goings all day long. And the kids! Yelling, shouting, running back and forth in front of our windows. It was too much. We decided to sell."

"Because they were too noisy?" I asked.

"No," she answered. "Because *we* were not."

They had felt left out. What was right for one time of life was wrong for another. It's impossible to stay in the past and stay happy.

In retirement, you should be able to take your house and your car or leave them. A good many prudent older people are deciding to leave them. One dollarwise retiree rationalized his decision this way: "I kept my car because I told myself it gave me a sense of freedom, even though I knew I could do without it. Now that I've sold it, I really feel free—free of expenses."

About his house, he said, "Because I'm over fifty-five, when I sold my house, I got the tax break of a lifetime—my profit of $60,000 was tax-free. That's sixty thousand reasons for giving up something I didn't need, anyway." (An individual may receive up to $100,000 of tax-free profit from the sale of his or her principal residence. This tax break for those over fifty-five can be taken advantage of in the sale of one house only.)

6. How to convince yourself that in retirement you don't have to take care of your ailing parents yourself

If you have ailing parents, you're likely to come face to face with one of the most tormenting decisions of your life. Should you keep them in your home, ministering to their needs with your time, your energy, and your love? Or should you send them off to the care of strangers in a nursing home or possibly to an apartment complex for the elderly?

Had you faced this decision in your family-building years and been fortunate enough to have your parents nearby, the following situation might have been yours.

The family was a three-part unit: the grandparents, the parents, and the grandchildren. The grandparents played an indispensable role in maintaining the stability and well-being of the family.

The grandparents were the cement that held the family together when marital misunderstanding and sibling rivalries threatened to split it apart. With the grandparents, the parents had a ceaseless source of counsel and help, a baby-sitting service, a caterer and private bank, and a hotel where no reservations were necessary and bills were never presented. The children experienced a brand of love like none other in the world. Through the grandparents, the children were linked to the family's past and trained to face the future with pride in their heritage. If grandparents didn't exist, the parents felt, they would have to be invented.

In that situation, it was very difficult for the middle-aged parents to refuse to care for the ailing grandparents with their own hands. The grandparents would have felt the bite of ingratitude and the bitterness of resentment. The children would have sensed their hurt and turned confused eyes to their parents. The parents would have found it hard to explain their feelings to the children, and their children's faith in them might have suffered a blow. The three-part structure, so necessary for the family's welfare, particularly the grandchildren's, would have collapsed.

If this was your situation, you had a deep-rooted need to keep the three-part family unit intact. In this case, if you decided it was best for you and your family as well as your parents, you might have cared for your ailing parents with the same touch-to-touch devotion that you lavished on your children.

But in retirement, you take over the grandparent role. The three-part family unit now consists of your grandchildren, your middle-aged children, and you and your spouse as grandparents. Your parents are no longer a part of it. Your obligation to take care of them yourself when they're ailing, based on your need to keep the three-part family unit intact, no longer exists.

Let's see what happens when you carry over that obligation into your retirement years.

Bringing ailing parents into your household means bringing in a network of restrictions. And at the time of your life when you should start living for yourself, that's unfair. "I'm just too old," a retired woman stated bluntly, "to start a family again." That is potentially what it could amount to.

What's more, if you're in your sixties, your parents are probably at least in their eighties; and that's the time senility and debilitating diseases are most likely to strike. You're not equipped to handle them. You do your severely ill parents a disservice, even harm, when you try to care for them with amateurish good intentions. The botched job you make of it fills you with frustration, resentment, and anger. "With my sick old father in the house," a sixty-two-year-old woman confessed, "I feel like somebody has just drained all the life out of me. I'm so furious. And I'm so guilty for feeling that way." The toll in emotional energy is more than you can stand.

There's no question about what to do when your parents are so ill that taking care of them yourself becomes an exercise in futility. Nursing homes for the aged, on the whole, aren't palaces; but there are pleasant ones and good ones, and the care your ailing parents get there is far better than the care you can provide. Take your unmanageable parents off your hands and put them into more capable ones.

This doesn't mean that under no circumstances should you take care of your ailing parents yourself. When you can give them the best possible care under your own roof without frustrating your retirement right to do what you please when you please, take care of them. It will give you great emotional satisfaction. Many mildly ill eighty-year-old parents are joys to have around. They are virtually self-sufficient, infectiously happy, considerate, gentle, and, above all, in complete empathy with your need to be yourself.

But when you can't give your ailing parents the best possible care at home, or when their crotchety demands rob you of your freedom, a medical institution would be the best place for them. You would no longer have to drain yourself of emotional energy playing the role of "the self-sacrificing son or daughter."

It could make a stunning difference in your life. A woman who had made the decision to transfer her ailing parent from her home to a nursing home writes: "This is the first time in thirty-two years my husband and I have been alone together, and we're having a ball putting our interests first. It's great, even better than before, because we now appreciate the luxury of it."

7. How to convince yourself that in retirement you don't have to live in total togetherness with your spouse

"We're a team," a middle-aged wife boasts. "We do everything together. We make our decisions together. We play together. We talk about each other's work experiences. Away from work, I wouldn't dream of doing anything without my husband, and he wouldn't dream of doing anything without me."

Togetherness has a sound basis. While the children are growing up, the husband and the wife must present a common front to give the children a sense of security. In a household where one spouse's authority is disputed by the other, the children are confused, directionless, and torn by conflicting loyalties. Togetherness is based on the parents' obligation to their children's welfare.

If togetherness stopped there, it would present no problem. But somehow it grows until it covers virtually every shareable facet of middle-aged married life. Spouses, even those without children, often seem to play the roles of "marriage partners," bound by an unwritten business contract to share and share alike almost all their thoughts and activities, to become carbon copies of each other. It is this overblown version of togetherness that has its drawbacks.

No two people think alike, like the same things, or act alike. To compress two people into a single mold is to squeeze out individuality. The middle-aged couple may look serene on the outside, but inside, each one may be feeling a loss of self, silently asking, Where's the real "me" gone? When will I do the things I've always wanted to do? What's happened to the person I've always wanted to be? They may feel threatened, troubled, or tense. Beneath the glossy surface of their apparent happiness, the real "mes" are struggling to break free.

No matter what your age, there's no longer the need to form a common front for the sake of the children after they are grown and leave home. The basis for total togetherness no longer exists, and you may want to stop the carbon-copy living that might have grown out of that togetherness. You no longer have to play the role of a full-fledged marriage partner. You can be a wife or a husband in the true sense—a person wedded to another but retaining one's own individuality. If you choose, you can do the things you want to do—alone. Instead of living in togetherness, you can live alone—together. You can usually do that only when you're young and have no children—or now, in retirement.

What happens when you carry over the responsibility of togetherness into retirement?

In middle age, togetherness is endurable because of a safety valve. Between nine and five of each working day, the marriage partners go their separate ways. But in retirement, they're with each other twenty-four hours a day, day after day after day. The French philosopher Jean-Paul Sartre portrayed his own version of hell in his play *No Exit:* a couple locked together forever in a single room. Togetherness in retirement often resembles Sartre's vision. "I feel like climbing walls," one wife of a retiree confessed. "We eat together, shop together, go out together. We're never out of each other's sight. I'd give anything if I could only get off by myself for a while."

Is togetherness a source of discord in your retirement marriage? Then stop being *we* and start being *me*. It could be the start of something big. Here's what's likely to happen.

When you recover your individuality, you realize that your spouse is an individual, too. You encourage him to be himself or her to be herself. The real "mes" that had been buried by middle-aged living emerge. You're two new people. It's almost as if you were meeting for the first time. Instead of being like each other, you can get to like each other. Marriage can become a new courtship. Free to do what you please when you please, you can be together; or you can each follow your own interests, alone or with others as the mood strikes you. This is a pattern of a successful love affair, and it can be yours in retirement marriage.

8. How to convince yourself that in retirement you don't have to be the kind of person your parents taught you to be

You are to a large extent what your parents made you. They were the first molders of your character. They did this to give you the preparation you needed to get along in the world. You might have accepted the responsibility to live your "in-the-world" years as the kind of person they taught you to be. They gave you a role to play in middle age, and you felt compelled to stay in character.

If you were fortunate, you were prepared for success. Your parents praised and encouraged you. They told you there was nothing you couldn't do. That made you more likely to enter your working and family-building life confident, self-reliant, industrious, unflappable, and unstoppable. That's a wonderful way to be. Be grateful to your parents for giving you the character that can make your retirement years successful.

If you were unfortunate, however, you were prepared just to get by. Your parents taught you to know your own limitations (not to reach for the moon) and to stay in your place. Their teaching methods were harsh; they deflated you or ignored you. That made you more likely to enter adult life timid and cautious, dependent on others, apathetic, and easily disconcerted and discouraged. You might not have known how to handle success because you never were prepared for it.

But in retirement, you're on your own. If you set out to walk the tightrope of retirement problems with the idea that you're going to fall, you'll fall—flat on your face. And there'll be nobody there to pick you up. You'll be in for a dismal old age.

Does your life have to turn out that way because of what your parents taught you a half century ago or more? It does not. Just realize this.

The character you have was given to you to help you through your working and family-building years. Those years are gone. You don't need that character anymore.

Toss it away. For the first time in your life, you can do it. You can do whatever you like without thinking, "Will my mother approve? Will my father approve?" The slate is wiped clean. You can look into yourself and find out the kind of person you really are. (You'll find a step-by-step guide for doing just that in the next chapter.) When you know yourself, you know your true potential and you can work at realizing it. Chances are, the new "me" will be the kind of person you've always wanted to be. And that kind of person will walk the retirement tightrope with confidence, courage, and success.

9. How to convince yourself that in retirement you don't have to redo your failures and successes to make them better

In middle age, you're impelled by the success drive.

It's a necessary motivation. You want to give the best to your growing children. You want to win in the fierce competition with your fellow workers and your fellow consumers. You're driven without letup to try to better your record.

One way of doing that is to look at the things you've done and rethink them. "I shoulda done this. I shoulda done that." Then use one or more of the "shouldas" to try to improve your successes as well as your failures.

That's a tremendous burden in middle age. In retirement, it could be a crushing one. You have all the successes and failures of your working and family-building life to redo.

Many retirees in their first years of retirement feel compelled to do just that. They take their old successes out of the closet and try to make them into greater successes. They try to correct the mistakes they have made over the past forty years or so. One woman writes: "In those first years after retirement, our lives were helter-skelter. We started new businesses, sold them, and started others. It was our business life all over again, but we wanted to do it better. We tried to set straight our sons' and daughters' tangled lives, for which we held ourselves responsible. We tried to turn our old business defeats— oh, how they rankled!—into victories. We tried to remake a whole lifetime. We clung to the tail of middle age, not realizing we had a tiger by the tail. . . . It was too much for us. We were miserable."

If you're one of those retirees who still play the role of the obsessive redoer, consider this Disney-like fable. It's an illustration of the old expression, You can't see the forest for the trees.

Think of your life before retirement as a journey through a forest thick with trees of every shape and variety. The trees are the events in your life.

As you travel through the forest, you stop at a stunted tree, a diseased tree, a tree that stopped growing almost at once, and at a tree that springs up to block your way. These trees are the failures in your life. They're the child who didn't turn out the way you had hoped, the promotion that slipped through your fingers, the plans for that farm that never got off the ground—all the things you set your heart on and never got.

You feel compelled to set things right—to make the stunted tree tall and the diseased tree well, to bring the stillborn tree to life, and to remove the tree that blocked your way.

You also halt before other kinds of trees. These are tall, strong, and vigorous. They're alive with the sounds of birds. These trees are your successes in life. They're the Ph.D. your child earned, the testimonial dinner your business associates gave you, the stock investments that paid off big—all the victories you've chalked up on your private scoreboard.

You feel an irresistible desire to make these trees even more beautiful. You prune them, water them, nourish them, and gather and plant their seeds.

Retirement comes. You're out of the woods. You look back. For the first time in your life, you see the forest. It's your middle-aged life as a whole. But you can no longer see the individual trees. The ugly trees and the beautiful trees have vanished from your life. From the vantage point of retirement, there are no middle-aged failures to turn into successes and no successes to make more successful. There is nothing to redo.

But a new journey lies ahead, potentially the most rewarding one of your life. Turn your face forward.

Now that you've rid yourself of your nine major middle-aged responsibilities, you're ready to learn two more guidelines for achieving emotional maturity. I'll show you how to uncover the real "me," which those responsibilities might have buried alive, and how to like the real me you uncover.

3

How to Know and Like Yourself in Retirement

The second guideline for achieving emotional maturity in retirement is

Know yourself.

You might never have been able to know yourself in middle age. Here's why.

For each of the nine responsibilities you assumed in middle age, you played a role. Review them. You were

1. a parent of growing children
2. a worker
3. a social conformist
4. a competitive consumer
5. a home-and-car owner
6. a self-sacrificing son or daughter
7. a marriage partner
8. a character molded by your parents
9. an obsessive redoer

In the theater of ancient times, all actors wore masks signifying their roles. Consider yourself in middle age as an actor wearing nine masks, one on top of the other. While you're wearing these masks, it's impossible to see yourself as you really are. To do so, these masks have to come off. And that's the main reason why you must get rid of your middle-aged responsibilities.

When you shed your middle-aged responsibilities, you drop your masks one by one. A strange creature is revealed. It's *you*. The real you. For perhaps the first time in quite some time, you have a chance to get reacquainted with yourself. What are you like?

Before you can answer that, you must understand what human emotions are. They make up the motivating force of our lives—driving us to go ahead, pushing us backward, and stopping us completely. They determine what we do, how we feel, what we want, and whether we get what we want. Our hates, loves, and fears are conditioned by our emotional structure. It gives us power or weakens us, operates for our benefit or our detriment, and causes us confusion or happiness.

Therefore, to know what you're like means to know how you react *emotionally* to people, things, and situations and to every problem they pose. You are the sum of your emotional reactions. In other words, you are what you feel.

Yet, if you're like most people of your generation, *you are not aware of most of your feelings*.

One reason is that as a child you might have been taught to suppress "unacceptable" feelings—exuberant ones, like excess joy, as well as depressive ones, like defeat. This early training has remained with you into retirement. Another reason is that in middle age, when you were playing all those roles, you were reacting like a cast of characters in a movie. Your emotions were those of the characters you played. You might never have known what you really felt.

So, don't be surprised if you have some difficulty now in recognizing just what you feel.

What you feel in retirement can be broken down into sixty basic emotions—thirty positive ones and thirty negative ones. These emotions make you *you*.

A good way to become acquainted with half of them is to go back to your answers to the retirement EQ quiz in chapter 1. Every yes answer indicates a negative emotion; every no answer, a positive one. To find out exactly which negative and positive emotions they are, on a separate sheet of paper, list all your answers to the retirement EQ quiz. See which negative or positive emotion corresponds to each answer.

KNOW YOUR RETIREMENT EMOTIONS

Retirement EQ Question	Negative emotion for yes answer	Positive emotion for no answer
1	Guilt	A feeling that you're doing the right thing
2	Irritability	A feeling that you can acclimate yourself to difficult situations without getting upset
3	Pressure	A feeling that you don't have to do what other people do

Retirement EQ Question	Negative emotion for yes answer	Positive emotion for no answer
4	Depression	A feeling of well-being
5	Fear	A feeling of faith in yourself
6	Close-mindedness	A feeling of open-mindedness
7	Low self-esteem	A feeling of self-respect
8	Boredom	A feeling of interest in people and things
9	Worry	A feeling that you can cope with your problems
10	Resentment	A feeling of acceptance that you must take precautions at this time of life
11	Anger	A feeling of being able to take things as they come

Retirement EQ Question	Negative emotion for yes answer	Positive emotion for no answer
12	Frustration	A feeling that you're fulfilling yourself in pursuing your interests
13	Selfishness	A feeling that you can spend your time the way you want
14	Envy	A feeling of contentment
15	Anxiety	A feeling that everything's going to be all right

Finished with your soul-searching? You might have made some unpleasant discoveries. You don't regard yourself as an envious person, do you? But your yes answer to question 14 reveals that you can be envious. You've never admitted that you can be afraid of anything, have you? But your yes answer to question 5 brings you face to face with your own fear.

Retirement problems can bring out the worst in you. You have to know what that worst is before you can do anything about it. Covering up your negative emotions is like refusing to admit you're ill. You let the virus attacking you destroy you. So face up to the negative emotions you have found; they're as much a part of you as your positive ones.

You have now found fifteen (out of thirty) of your dominant positive and negative emotions. But that's only half of the emotions that motivate your retirement life. To find the other half, sit down when nobody's around and think of a retirement problem you faced recently. What emotion did you feel? Was it one of the emotions listed in the Know Your Retirement Emotions chart? If it was not, look for the emotion in the following chart. It contains an additional fifteen positive and fifteen negative emotions likely to be triggered by retirement problems.

| THIRTY MORE RETIREMENT EMOTIONS ||
Your Negative Emotion	Your Positive Emotion
16 Hate	A feeling that love and understanding is the better way to cope with life
17 Maliciousness	A feeling that you like to talk about the good things in people
18 Discouragement	A feeling of determination to go on even when things go wrong
19 Self-pity	A feeling that it's wrong to put yourself down

Your Negative Emotion	Your Positive Emotion
20 Wanting to alibi	A feeling that it's right to face the music
21 Insecurity	A feeling that you can rely on yourself even in the tightest spots
22 Hypocrisy	A feeling that sincerity pays off
23 Temper	A feeling that you're in control of yourself at all times
24 Revenge	A feeling that it's best to let bygones be bygones
25 Impulsiveness	A feeling that you can avoid pitfalls if you look before you leap
26 Aggressiveness	A feeling that you get more by cooperating than by fighting
27 Miserliness	A feeling of joy in giving

Your Negative Emotion	Your Positive Emotion
28 Grouchiness	A feeling that you can take life's little troubles without fuss or feathers
29 Inferiority	A feeling that just being yourself makes you as good as anybody
30 Discourtesy	A feeling of regard for other people's feelings

You won't get a complete list of fifteen additional emotions at the first sitting. Or the second. Or the third. Keep trying. It will start your thought process working on its own. Revealing insights about your emotions will come to you in the middle of the night, while you're taking a walk, during your trip to the supermarket—almost anytime. Keep a pen or pencil handy and jot them down.

Here's another way to discover your emotions. When you're in the throes of wrestling with a retirement problem, stop and think, "What do I really feel?"

For example, if your daughter calls up at five-thirty and announces, "Mom, I'm bringing the kids over for dinner in half an hour," do you smile on the outside and simmer on the inside? What's the simmering caused by? Self-pity? Irritability? Anger? Guilt? Don't hide your negative emotions. You might have done that all your life. Bring them out in the open and label them.

You'll find that as your list grows, it will also change.

Who you think you are and who you really are may be two different persons. You may credit yourself with positive emotions that, in the face of real life, simply don't exist. (You don't really enjoy giving *that* much, do you?) You may saddle yourself with negative emotions that seldom are activated. (Take that bad temper of yours you're so afraid of; when did you really blow your top last?) Modify your listings as reality reveals you more and more to yourself, like a photographic print in a developing solution.

When you feel certain you've got a clear picture of yourself, see how it compares with the picture your spouse has of you. If you're frank with your spouse, you'll be shocked to find how frank your spouse will be with you. You may have to rush back to your list and start some heavy revisions. Nothing helps you see yourself more clearly than when you look at yourself through the eyes of someone close who loves you.

In a few weeks, the list of your dominant positive and negative emotions will be complete. If it doesn't look like the thirty most desirable traits imaginable, don't go into hiding. Nobody else's list is any better. People who do not have tempers, who do not get angry, who do not get jealous, who do not get frightened, do not exist. It's human nature to have negative emotions.

"All right," you finally concede. "I admit I have negative emotions. Now, how do I get rid of them?"

Face a hard fact: You can't.

Saints can, but most of us aren't saints.

What you can do is put your negative emotions to work for you. When a judo expert is attacked, he or she uses the strength of the assailant to win the fight. That's what you're going to do. You're going to use the emotional energy generated by your negative emotions to help solve your retirement problems. You're going to practice emotional judo.

But you'll be ready to do it only when you learn to

Like yourself.

And that's the third guideline for achieving emotional maturity in retirement.

What does liking yourself mean? Just this—that you accept the whole of you, your positive emotions and your negative emotions, and put your stamp of approval on the complete package.

Getting to like yourself can be as easy as running your eyes down your list of positive and negative emotions and saying, "That's me! And I like me!" Or it can be one of the most difficult jobs you've ever faced. You can't hide your negative emotions any longer. You're painfully aware that they're there. You feel guilty for having them. You're afraid of the harm they may do you. You look at your list and exclaim with disgust, "That's me? What's there to like?"

If you start off not liking yourself, it may not be your fault. Your parents and your teachers might have instilled in you a bad image of yourself. The roles you were forced to play in middle age (particularly if you didn't play them well) might have left you feeling inadequate. People and circumstances might have combined to brainwash you into the habit of not liking yourself.

Now's the time to kick that habit. The past is behind you. You're starting fresh. Start to like yourself. Begin today.

"That's easier said than done," one retiree complained. "You can no more say, 'Today I'll start liking myself,' than you can say, 'Today I'll give up smoking,' and expect it to happen easily. It just won't work."

That's right. It won't—unless you back up your resolution to like yourself with a program designed to help you carry that resolution out successfully. It has to be a program that will motivate you, encourage you, and stimulate you. A simple program. Something that's feasible. And, above all, a program that's fun. The happiest retirees I know assure me that finding happiness is a game. That's why I've developed a program that's actually an exciting game to help you like yourself. So start now to play.

THE LEARN-TO-LIKE-YOURSELF GAME

This is the idea behind the program. When you don't like yourself, you simply don't give yourself credit for all the good things you do. You not only belittle them ("Oh, that was nothing. Anybody could do that.") but also actually wash them out of your mind. If I asked you at the end of the day to tell me about all the good things you did all day long, you'd say, "Honestly, not one."

The object of the game is to get you more and more aware of all the good things you do and to keep score of them. As your score mounts, so will your self-respect. In just a few weeks, you may look in the mirror and say, "Old friend, I'm proud of you!" Without grueling effort, you'll have learned how to like yourself.

Here's how to play the learn-to-like-yourself game.

HOW TO SCORE POINTS

Every time you do something good, you score a point. What's "something good"?

Did you tell your wife how nice her dress looked?

That's something good.

Did you call the butcher to tell him what a fine roast he sent you?

That's something good.

Did you go to the library to pick up a book your husband wanted to read?

That's something good.

Little things? Sure. But it's out of these little things that you build your daily happiness. Every time you do something good, you feel good. When you're in the habit of not liking yourself, you won't let yourself feel good, and that's why you think those good, little things you do don't count. They do count. Your chance to do big things doesn't come along every day, but little things are part and parcel of your life. Every good, little thing you become aware of doing brings you one point closer to liking yourself.

HOW TO ENTER YOUR SCORE ON THE SCOREBOARD

At the end of the day, find a quiet spot where you can be alone with a diary. Stretch out, relax, let your hair down, and turn on some soft music. These moments are going to be the highlight of your day. You're going to confide to a diary all the good, little things you did from the time you got up in the morning. Boast. Brag. Have a wonderful time. You've earned it.

A sixty-three-year-old woman described her moments with her diary this way: "Going over the day in my mind is like walking in a garden. Recalling all the good things I've done is like picking roses."

When you've finished reliving your happy moments and entering them in your diary, count up the number of good, little things you did during the day. Take a red pencil or crayon and write that number in your diary. Make it three or four times larger than your normal writing. Draw a huge red circle around it. All this is to remind you that every day is a red-letter day when you're learning to like yourself.

Your diary is your scoreboard. And you've just entered your daily score.

HOW TO KNOW WHEN YOU WIN THE GAME

At the end of the week, add up your daily scores. What's the winning figure?

Most retirees who start off by not liking themselves predict a first week's score of 2 or 3. If you're one of those retirees, you'll be pleasantly surprised to learn that your first week's score is likely to hover around 50! That's 47 or 48 more happy incidents than you expected.

But that doesn't mean you've won. You start winning only when your score grows bigger and bigger week after week.

Happiness is what you're after. When you realize the potential little things have to make you happy, you'll make a conscious effort to do more and more good ones. And the more good things you do for people, the more you'll like yourself. In six weeks or so, your dislike of yourself may be ancient history. The morning will come when you can look in the mirror and see the beaming face of someone you like.

SOME HINTS FOR IMPROVING YOUR GAME

You can rack up more points and rack them up faster by following certain guidelines:

Build a good mental image of yourself. Describe in your mind the person you've always dreamed of being. Is that person loving? charming? enthusiastic? magnetic? courteous? sympathetic? kind? Then work hard at making that dream come true.

Take a guided tour down memory lane. You're the guide, and the only things you're going to point out to yourself are the good things you've done in your life. Do you remember how you rushed a sick friend to the hospital the night of a blizzard? how you tutored your neighbor's kid in algebra so that he could graduate from high school? how you made the girl who was to become your wife fall in love with you? If you were capable of doing likable things then, you're capable of doing other likable things now. Do them.

Avoid people who tear you down as you would a typhoid carrier. Until you've learned to like yourself, these people can reinforce your belief that you're a pretty miserable creature. Avoid people who are critical, malicious, and jealous, and who never have a good word for you. Don't even go to a restaurant where the headwaiter looks down his nose. Stay away from that sharp-tongued bank clerk who always makes you feel like two cents. And watch out particularly for those who tear you down indirectly. These are the frustrated and depressed ones whose moodiness and mental turmoil are contagious, and who drag you down to their own abysmal level of self-respect just by being with you.

Since you can't banish everyone who is harmful to you, remember that if you let what you feel about yourself depend on what others feel about you, you're putting yourself at their mercy. Don't expect any. Fight back. If they attack you directly, tell them in so many words what they can do with their opinions. If they unconsciously try to hurt you with harmful attitudes, tell them to wise up to themselves. Don't be afraid to hurt feelings. You're bound to. But don't blame yourself. What you're doing you're doing in self-defense.

Once you learn how to like yourself, you won't have to give these assassins of self-respect a second thought. That's because liking yourself is an unbreakable habit. They couldn't make you dislike yourself again no matter how hard they tried.

Reward yourself. Decide to give yourself a special treat if your score this week is higher than it was last week—a dinner at a good restaurant, a new scarf, or a ticket to the ball game. Choose anything that you wouldn't ordinarily give yourself. It's a tangible sign of victory, and it spurs you on to try harder. It also helps keep you going on those days when everything seems to go wrong and you find yourself tempted to slip back into self-dislike. You can fight off that temptation because you know that when you do, there'll be a reward waiting for you at the end of the week.

There's another reason for rewarding yourself. It gets you into the habit of being good to yourself. And that's what liking yourself is all about.

When you like yourself, you want to do good things for yourself.

RESULTS OF WINNING THE LEARN-TO-LIKE-YOURSELF GAME

When you like yourself, you do one of the best things you can for yourself—you resolve to let your negative emotions go to work for you. You begin to understand that if you let your negative emotions continue to work against you, you will not be able to cope with your retirement problems. Now you can live with those negative emotions of yours that disgusted you. They can help you rather than hurt you. So, you don't have to be afraid of them, and you don't have to feel guilty for having them.

Now you're ready to practice emotional judo. You're ready to use your negative emotions to help beat your retirement problems. How? In the next chapter, you'll learn how to follow the final guideline to achieve emotional maturity for retirement.

4

How to Make Decisions That Solve Retirement Problems

Do you recall the unhappy spouses in chapter 1? Their negative emotions were aroused because the retired husband hung around the house all day. But they didn't realize they had a problem; they thought they were just "getting old." So they just let things happen, and their negative emotions ran riot.

The happy couple felt the same negative emotions. That made them realize they had a problem, that those negative emotions could hurt them, and they decided to do something. What was that "something"? Just this—they knew they had to come to a decision concerning their problem, and they got started on working toward one. They used their negative emotions to attack their problem instead of letting their negative emotions attack them.

The unhappy couple didn't like themselves and did nothing good for themselves. The happy couple liked themselves and did the best thing they could for themselves: They practiced emotional judo.

When you like yourself, you have the ability to do the same thing. The technique is as simple as ABC.

    a. Realize that when a negative emotion surfaces, you're face to face with a problem.

    b. Say to yourself, "If I don't try to solve this problem, my negative emotions will take over and I'll be hurt."

    c. Use the emotional energy generated by your negative emotions to get started on making a decision concerning your problem.

That brings us to the fourth and final guideline for achieving emotional maturity in retirement.

Make decisions.

What's so extraordinary about that? Haven't you been making decisions all your working and family-building life?

Take a deep breath. You're possibly in for a shock.

You may not have made many decisions in the principal areas of your life.

Once you settled down to middle-aged living, you played nine major roles. Only very creative actors playing roles make decisions to change them; usually, however, they follow the script. Possibly, so did you.

Your script was unwritten but nonetheless real. It was prepared for you by your parents, your bosses, your family, and your peer group. It was they who might have actually made the decisions for you—you simply carried out their stage directions.

You had the illusion you were making decisions, but look back. What major choices did you have? Did you decide whether to buy a car? a house? live near a school? take the whole family on vacations? build a pool in the backyard? If you could afford it, you did it—and often even if you couldn't afford it. You had little choice. Didn't you usually do what your peer group did? Didn't you usually share virtually all your nonwork time with your marriage partner? Didn't you feel you had to care for your ailing parents? You might not have dared to say, "No. I want to do things my way."

Some exceptions. You did make decisions of key importance if you were an executive or a manager, a professional person, or a free-lance artist or writer. No matter what your occupation, you did make on-the-job decisions. But your decisions were limited to your field of expertise. Away from it, you most likely played the nine major roles of middle age. You might have made key decisions on the design of a multimillion-dollar aircraft, but you still might have had no choice when it came to playing golf with your business associates.

Didn't the roles you played permit you to make any decisions at all? Of course, they did. Mashed potatoes or boiled? Red trim on your car or gold? Schlitz or Miller's? Minor decisions that created no problems. You could live with one solution as easily as with another. These are simplified examples, of course. But within the areas of your life covered by your nine major middle-aged roles, the problem areas, you might never have been really called on to make a decision of your own.

In retirement, you encounter fifteen new key problem areas. The decisions provided by your middle-aged roles are now useless and possibly harmful. For perhaps the first time since your youth, you have to make all the decisions, major and minor. But decision-making ability is like all your abilities—if you don't use it, you lose it. And in most areas of your life, you haven't used your decision-making power for decades. Retirement is an age of decisions, and you may enter it powerless.

"Do you know what the worst part about retirement is?" a former machine-shop foreman groaned. "Decisions."

"Didn't you make decisions on the job?" I asked.

"Sure, but that was technical. Like doing a crossword puzzle. Retirement problems are different, emotional."

"What do you do about them?"

"I find excuses not to do anything about them. I put them off. When I'm in a bind, I try to get other people to make them for me."

"Why?"

"To tell the truth, I just don't know how to make a decision."

It's small wonder that so many retirees flock to retirement communities, where decisions are made for them. But if you want a successful retirement on your own, you must learn how to make decisions. Here's how.

TEN STEPS FOR MAKING A SUCCESSFUL DECISION IN RETIREMENT
---

1. **Gather all the facts.** That may take legwork as well as mental effort. Go to it—you've got the time.

2. **Apply reason to the facts and come up with a number of possible decisions.** Don't get hung up on the myth that there's only one solution to a problem. Nothing's cut-and-dried. Every problem can be solved in several ways.

3. **Eliminate any decision based on your middle-aged responsibilities.** You've outgrown those responsibilities. You don't want to take a step backward, do you?

THE NEXT STEP IS THE KEY STEP.

4. **From several possible decisions, pick the one that gives you the most emotional satisfaction.** You

can do this only when you like yourself. Then you want only the best for yourself, which means the most emotional satisfaction you can get. Your positive emotions should now take over and guide you to the decision that gives it to you. (Do you see now why liking yourself is so important? It puts your negative emotions to work for you to start you on the solution to your retirement problems and your positive emotions to work to complete the solution.)

Your retirement problems are not technical problems (such as you had on the job) that can be solved solely on the basis of reason. Your retirement problems are basically emotional, and your final decisions concerning them are made emotionally.

5. Accept the fact that your decision involves compromise or even sacrifice. Every decision is reached after weighing the pros and the cons. Don't get upset because the decision you've arrived at has its quota of cons. It's the overall result you're looking for; a beautiful forest is not ruined by a few deformed trees.

6. Never test your decision by asking other people's opinions. Your decision will get you something you want, not something somebody else wants. Take another's opinion, and you take on another's desires. That's the same as being somebody else. If you like yourself, you want to be yourself.

7. Once you make your decision, leave it at that. Sure, there were other possible solutions, and you can drive yourself dizzy by agonizing over whether you picked the right one or the wrong one. Your positive emotions go to work for you. Have confidence in them.

8. Put your decision into action immediately, with vigor and enthusiasm. The best way to scotch doubts is to swing into action and play to win. Any athlete will tell you that's the only way to win. But remember, you can't win 'em all. Making a decision doesn't mean your troubles are over. You could make a wrong decision.

9. **If your decision proves wrong, take it calmly and try to determine what went wrong (so that you won't make the same mistake again).** Chances are, your emotional responses were right; something else must have gone wrong. Did you collect all the facts? Did you make an error or two thinking them through? A quiet hour or so with a pencil and paper may help. And a wrong decision isn't always worthless. There are often ways to get something of value out of one. Put your ingenuity to work. Dale Carnegie, author of *How to Win Friends and Influence People*, advises, "When you come up with a lemon, make lemonade."

10. **When you've made the wrong decision, have the gumption to start all over again.** Where do you get the gumption? From liking yourself. When you like yourself, you won't hurt yourself and let a defeat get you down. You'll rebound naturally and keep on trying. The next time around, you'll probably come up with the right decision.

Here's a story of how one woman used her negative emotions and the ten steps to come to a decision regarding her retirement problem. It's the kind of problem that could very well come your way.

Recently, I met an old friend at a motor court. He had been retired for a few years. He told me he was traveling around "just for the hell of it."

I said, "Is Emily enjoying it?" Emily is his wife. He replied, "She's not with me."

I was shocked. Emily and John are one of the closest couples I know.

"She's not sick?" I inquired.

"Oh, no. Never been healthier."

"Well, then, what's happened to you two?"

He hesitated. Then he said, "You and I are old friends. I can tell you about it."

All his working life, he explained, he had wanted to drive around the country, just following his nose. Soon after he retired, he took his first trip. His wife went along. She tried to grin and bear it, but it was obvious she wasn't having the time of her life. She said nothing during the trip, but when they came home, she let him know how she felt.

"I was cold," she said. "I didn't sleep well. The food was awful. I felt like a gypsy. Another day in that car and I would have screamed! I hated the trip. And I hated you for taking me."

She spoke calmly. She was in complete control of herself. That's because she had everything worked out in her own mind. This is how she did it: On the way home, she recognized from the miserable way she felt that she had a problem. She put all the emotional energy churning up inside her to work to get her started on solving that problem. She sifted the facts, thought them over, and came up with some possible decisions concerning her husband's future trips.

One decision was "It's my duty to do things with my husband, so I better get to like it." But she realized that that decision was based on middle-aged togetherness, and she discarded it. From the several possible decisions left her, she picked the one that gave her the most emotional satisfaction. She told it to John.

"Look, honey," she said, "If I go again, I'm going to boil over like an overheated motor. I'm going to have a rotten time, so you're going to have a rotten time. It makes no sense. The next time the wanderlust strikes you, I'm off to Cape Cod. When you feel you've had enough, pick me up at my hotel and we'll go home together."

It was a tough decision for her to make. They had never been separated before in their married life, and she knew she would miss him terribly. But she liked herself, and she knew her positive emotions could guide her only to a decision that, all in all, would be good for her. Besides, he would get what he wanted, his dream trips, with her blessing.

She didn't allow any doubts to cross her mind. If her decision went sour, she knew she could start all over again and come up with another decision. And if that decision didn't work, she'd try again. Liking herself gave her the courage and the will to keep on trying.

"At least," her husband protested, "talk to Fran and Harold about it and see what they think." But she wanted none of that. Nobody could feel what she felt; nobody could know what gave her emotional satisfaction. It was her decision to make and nobody else's. So despite her husband's protests, of which there were many that went on for some time, she stuck to her guns. And the next time he drove off into the sunset, she took a plane to Cape Cod.

It ended happily. The small vacations they have from each other make them ardent lovers when they get back together again.

This woman was emotionally mature for retirement. And you?

ARE YOU EMOTIONALLY MATURE FOR RETIREMENT?

THE FIRST GUIDELINE

Have you gotten rid of your middle-aged responsibilities; that is to say, have you shed your middle-aged roles to unmask the real you?

THE SECOND GUIDELINE

Have you gotten to know yourself by listing all your positive and negative emotions aroused by your retirement problems?

THE THIRD GUIDELINE

Have you gotten to like yourself—negative emotions and all? Do you feel able to put your negative emotions to work for you to start the decision-making process and your positive emotions to work for you to make your decisions?

THE FOURTH GUIDELINE

Do you make decisions using the ten steps for making a successful decision in retirement?

Four yes answers mean you've followed the four guidelines for achieving emotional maturity for retirement. If you've followed them successfully, you should be able to solve your retirement problems under most circumstances. When you take your retirement EQ quiz again, you should score 10 on every question and boost your score to 150. You've grown into an emotionally mature retiree.

Decision making can be agonizingly slow. It's not hard to see why. When you have a choice of several decisions, the one you should select is the one that gives you the most emotional satisfaction. But how do you know which decision does that? Frequently, the lines of communication between our feelings and our awareness of them is clogged with static. The static represents all sorts of practical and reasonable considerations. Too often, we're partially deaf to our own emotional messages; our emotional ear is malfunctioning from disuse. In short, the emotional message may have to fight its way through to our consciousness. That takes time. And that's why even the emotionally mature person often deliberates for days —even weeks—before making a choice.

When you're emotionally mature, you let your positive emotions go to work for you to select the most emotionally satisfying decision (step 4). That sounds vague and intangible. It isn't. Your positive emotions form your emotional outlook—a sharp, clear statement of how you feel about a situation, a person, or a thing. This is your attitude. When you're emotionally mature, you form emotionally mature attitudes. These attitudes have been built by your positive emotions to give you the most emotional satisfaction.

When you have several choices, make your decision based on your emotionally mature attitude. When you're aware of your emotionally mature attitude, you don't have to waste as much time in agonizing pondering.

There is a separate emotionally mature attitude for each of the fifteen key problem areas of retirement, and these attitudes differ radically from the attitudes you held in these areas during your middle years. If you're just starting to make the emotional transition from middle age to retirement age (if you are retiring early, you face many of the same problems), you are not yet aware of the new emotionally mature attitudes that can solve your problems. To discover them by yourself, you would have to solve dozens of retirement problems by the ten-step program in each key problem area.

But don't let that upset you. Sociological research, including my own, has pinpointed the emotionally mature retirement attitudes. In the next two chapters, I'll tell you what they are and how to put them to work for you to help you get what you want from yourself, from others, and from life in general.

5

How to Get What You Want from Yourself and Other People

Do you know what you want in retirement? Just for the fun of it, take a few minutes and make a list.

Now let's find out what you really want. Just answer yes or no to the questions in this short questionnaire.

WHAT DO YOU WANT IN RETIREMENT?

1. A good relationship with your children?

2. Peace of mind concerning your health and that of your spouse?

3. The right kind of friends for your retirement years?

4. A better marriage than before with the same spouse?

5. No decrease in brainpower and possibly an increase?

6. *The kind of* self-improvement *that makes you look better on the outside and feel better on the inside?*

7. *A new* image *that younger people will respect (to replace the one you lost when you began to look old)?*

8. *Pleasurable use of your* free *time?*

9. *A way to get the most out of your shrunken* money *supply?*

10. *The kind of* food *that's best for you?*

11. *A* home *that meets your retirement needs without restricting your freedom?*

12. *A* hobby *that's right for you in retirement?*

13. *The kind of job you need in retirement if you decide to go back to* work?

14. *Travel in order to break out of your retirement shell?*

15. *A maximum of* safety *with a minimum of* fear?

Every yes indicates a want. And if you're like most people who take this quiz, you'll have checked off fifteen yes answers. Chances are, the list you made up before didn't contain more than half your wants.

Each stage of life comes with its own package of wants. Some of the wants in it are familiar; some of them novel. In retirement, you get a new package of wants. But if you were still clinging to emotional middle age when you made up your list, you hadn't opened the package.

Now you have, by answering the questionnaire. You know the fifteen basic wants of retirement.

But there is often an enormous gap between wanting and getting what you want. That's why researchers in the field have designated these fifteen wants as the fifteen key problem areas of retirement. The words they use to identify these areas are printed in roman in the questionnaire: children, health, friends, marriage, brainpower, self-improvement, image, free time, money, food, home, hobby, work, travel, and safety.

You had a glimpse of some of the problems in these areas when you took the retirement EQ quiz. There are tougher problems ahead. When you solve your retirement problems, you get what you want. And the fastest, surest way to solve your problems is to make decisions based on your emotionally mature attitudes.

In this chapter, I'll introduce you to the first seven emotionally mature attitudes, those that will help you get what you want from yourself and other people in the key problem areas of children, health, friends, marriage, brainpower, self-improvement, and your image (the way younger people see you).

I'll pose a typically difficult problem in each of these areas and give you three possible decisions to choose from. Select the decision you feel will give you what you want. Then read on to find out what your emotionally mature attitude in that key problem area should be and what decision you should have arrived at had you put that attitude to work for you. Compare your decision with the correct one.

If you failed to select the right decision, it's because you didn't have the right attitude for that problem area. Try not to let that happen in real life. If you come across a problem in the area in which you've failed, remember what your emotionally mature retirement attitude should be and apply it.

Here's your first problem. It's based, like all the others, on a true situation.

Problem Area Number One: Children

You want *a good relationship with your children.*

YOUR SPECIFIC PROBLEM

You've moved to smaller quarters. Your income is down. You have a married daughter. She has a ten-year-old boy and a four-year-old girl. Your daughter comes to you and says, "Mom, I want a divorce. But I can get one only if you help me."

She'd like money for the divorce and money to live on while she's looking for a job. She'd like to move in with you and bring the kids along. She'd like you to take care of the kids while she's out job hunting and dating.

You have to do something.

YOUR DECISION

1. Give her all the help she asks for, no matter how much it costs in dollars and distress.

2. Give her no help at all, even though you're able to.

3. Help her by doing only those things that don't hurt you.

HOW TO GET WHAT YOU WANT

Don't apply your middle-aged attitude: My children come first all the time and at all costs. Reject decision 1.

Do apply your emotionally mature retirement attitude: My spouse and I come first, but I'll do as much as I can in an emergency without jeopardizing our happiness.

Based on this new attitude, your emotionally mature retirement decision is

3. Help her by doing only those things that don't hurt you.

Tell her, "I'm sorry, but the strain of having two kids in a small apartment day in and day out is too much for me. But I will baby-sit when you need me."

Explain that you have some money you can spare, but it's not very much. Suggest she look for a job first and then get the divorce.

"You're grown up, and you must realize it. You must learn to rely on yourself and take care of yourself. Your father and I have our own lives to lead." One retiree in a similar situation warned her daughter, "I'm not playing God anymore."

As a result of your decision and your explanation of it, your daughter will realize you're not the "Mom" and Dad's not the "Pop" of her growing-up years. She'll see you both as human beings with your own hopes and needs. She'll understand that she'll have to learn to become an individual, too, and not be a dependent child.

The friction caused by your desire to lead your own life and your daughter's desire to have you lead hers (at great sacrifice to yourself) will vanish. A new kind of relationship will spring up between you based on mutual liking and respect for each other as persons, a friendship strengthened by blood ties. That's the good relationship with your children you want in retirement.

Problem Area Number Two: Health

You want *peace of mind concerning your health and that of your spouse.*

YOUR SPECIFIC PROBLEM

You were a poor boy. In middle age you made a great deal of money. You couldn't enjoy it because your work load was so heavy. You've just retired. Now you can travel first-class, dine in four-star restaurants, and stay at deluxe hotels. Your first superluxury trip is booked, and you're ready to go. Your wife becomes ill.

You have to do something.

YOUR DECISION

1. Don't let her stand in the way of realizing your dream. Go yourself and leave her at home.
2. Cancel the trip until she's ready to go—and help take care of her in the meantime.
3. Take her on the trip, just as if she were well.

HOW TO GET WHAT YOU WANT

Don't apply your middle-aged attitude: The chance of any serious illness striking me or my spouse is small. Reject decision 3. (The retiree who actually faced this problem didn't. He took his wife along and saw her hospitalized in Istanbul. He paid for his emotional immaturity with a ruined trip, a wife in worsened condition, and a hangover of remorse, guilt, and anxiety.)

Do apply your emotionally mature retirement attitude: Serious illness can strike anytime, and I will care for my afflicted spouse if it does.

Based on this new attitude, your emotionally mature retirement decision is

2. Cancel the trip until she's ready to go—and help take care of her in the meantime.

Your new attitude toward health does two things for you. First, it directs you to stop hiding the fact that you and your wife can become seriously ill. You learn to bring it out into the open, live with it, and take it in your stride; it's part of life. Second, it prepares you to give of yourself gladly to take care of your wife in sickness as you would have her take care of you, even though it means giving up things that are important to you. You assume a new responsibility that you will never shed.

In short, with this attitude, you're emotionally conditioned to face the potentiality of the worst happening and to make sacrifices willingly and unstintingly if it does. When you can face the possibility of tragedy and be ready to do what has to be done if it comes, you have achieved peace of mind. That's the peace of mind concerning health that you want in retirement.

However, never let your acceptance of the fact that you and your spouse can become seriously ill obsess you, as it does many retirees. If you do, you become overconscious of your body. Every ache and pain seems a signal of the onset of a debilitating or mortal disease. You are on constant alert for signs of multiple sclerosis, kidney disease, cancer, heart disease, cystic fibrosis, Parkinson's disease, muscular dystrophy, and the rest. Even when you're feeling great, you believe you need continual monitoring and support by health professionals. You start a new career—going to doctors. Once you're on the medical merry-go-round, it's almost impossible to get off.

If you're a victim of this disease obsession, or if you think you have a tendency toward it, here's what to do.

Start with a look at the cheering health statistics for the nation's over-sixties. The great majority of retirees, more than 96 percent of them, are abundantly healthy. That makes the odds twenty-five to one against a major disease striking you or your spouse.

Then lengthen those odds by following seven simple health rules. Here they are (as worked out by a California medical research study).

- Eat breakfast.
- Eat three square meals a day and avoid snacking.
- Get seven to eight hours sleep every night.
- Get moderate exercise two or three times a week.
- Keep your weight within normal limits.

- Drink in moderation or not at all.
- Don't smoke.

That's all there is to it. Naturally, if you're disease-obsessed, you can't have peace of mind concerning health. You can when you rule that obsession out of your life.

When you follow the seven simple health rules, or any equivalent set of rules, you'll get a buoyant sense of physical well-being. And that will add to your peace of mind concerning health in retirement.

Problem Area Number Three: Friends

You want *the right kind of friends for your retirement years*.

YOUR SPECIFIC PROBLEM

Your husband has been retired for two years. Your social life is only a shadow of what it was before his retirement. Out of boredom, he registers for a course in figure drawing. In class he meets a forty-five-year-old married woman. She's a professional book designer and active in local politics and the consumer movement. Your husband finds her world new and exciting. They meet frequently over a cup of coffee. "I can really talk to her," he tells you. "We understand each other."

Your friends and relatives feel that his conduct is disgraceful.

You have to do something.

YOUR DECISION

1. Say, "I'm glad you have an interesting friend."
2. Start looking for a "boyfriend."

3. Arrange for a full schedule of social activities with couples in your own age group to remind him who his friends really are.

HOW TO GET WHAT YOU WANT

Don't apply your middle-aged attitude: The right friends for me are couples in my age group with whom I share my social life. Reject decision 3.

Do apply your emotionally mature retirement attitude: My friends can be of any age or sex as long as I can share my intimate thoughts and emotions with them and rely on them to be my channels to the outside world of nonretirement activities.

Based on this new attitude, your emotionally mature retirement decision is

1. Say, "I'm glad you have an interesting friend."

You're freer now to derive more from friendship than just a good time. You can experience, as you might not have been able to do in middle age, the deep emotional satisfaction that comes with the sharing of intimate thoughts and feelings. You can achieve a profound understanding with another person that neither time nor distance can erase. "If my friend was a thousand miles away for a year," one retired woman explained, "I could talk to her when she came back as if she'd only stepped out of the room for a minute."

This is the kind of close friendship you might have had when you were very much younger and always wished you could have again. You can.

But in retirement, that kind of friendship cannot make you completely happy as it stands. It needs an added ingredient. Let a retired advertising man explain.

"Retirement is like being shut away from what's happening. I want my friends to be channels to the outside world. I want them to make me feel that I'm in the thick of things again. That's why I make friends with people who are doing things. I don't care if they're young. I don't care if they're old. I don't care if they're men or women. What I do care about is that through them I can feel the pulse of things again. That makes my pulse beat faster."

In this problem, your husband found a close friend who supplied that added ingredient for retirement happiness. It should give you hope that you can, too. Not a "boyfriend," not a sexual partner. But a man or woman of any age who will satisfy your need for a strong emotional attachment and who will connect you with the excitement and stimulation of the world outside your retirement shell. When you find such a person, that's the friend you want in retirement—the right kind of friend. (See chapter 10 for the emotionally mature attitude that will help you make a real friend.)

Problem Area Number Four: Marriage

You want *a better marriage than before with the same spouse.*

YOUR SPECIFIC PROBLEM

Your husband has set up a hobby workshop in the basement. When he was at home before his retirement, you were able to talk to him about anything that popped into your head whenever it popped into your head. He was always warm and receptive. But now when you barge into his workshop to chat with him—at least a dozen times a day—he gets angry. You feel terrible.

You have to do something.

YOUR DECISION

1. Find some way of getting your thoughts through to him without disturbing him while he's busy.

2. Have a heart-to heart talk with him, reminding him that marriage is sharing and that he can't act like a bachelor while he's living with a wife.

3. Be as independent as he is and stop sharing your thoughts with him.

HOW TO GET WHAT YOU WANT

Don't apply your middle-aged attitude: I share as many nonwork activities with my spouse as possible. Reject decision 2.

Do apply your emotionally mature retirement attitude: My husband and I are both individuals with the right to do our own thing without interference from each other.

Based on this new attitude, your emotionally mature retirement decision is

1. Find some way of getting your thoughts through to him without disturbing him while he's busy.

One woman solved this problem by pinning up her thoughts on a bulletin board. "When my husband finishes whatever he's doing, he takes them down and reads them.

"In that way, I let him do what he wants to do without butting in. He realizes I have the same right. When I have my friends over during the day, just as I used to before he retired, he stays out of sight.

"What does he do after he reads what I put up on the bulletin board? When we're all relaxed—sometimes when we're taking a walk after dinner—he talks about the notes. He doesn't feel obliged to talk. He wants to. That's a lot different. Our talks are warmer. They're deeper. We draw a lot closer together."

When you restrict each other's freedom in retirement marriage, tension results. There's nothing like tension to close down communication. Without communication, no marriage can succeed at any age.

As a result of your attitude, you will accept his right to do his own thing, and he will accept yours. The tension will be removed, and when that happens, the lines of communication will open up again. This sense of freedom is likely to make your conversations flow even more easily and take on greater meaning. You may get to know each other better and care for each other more. And that's the better marriage you want with the same spouse in retirement.

Problem Area Number Five: Brainpower

You want *no decrease in brainpower and possibly an increase.*

YOUR SPECIFIC PROBLEM

You've been retired for two years. You've spent that time lazing on your porch and playing golf. You tell everybody how happy you are that you don't have to put your brain to work anymore solving all those technical problems on the job. Your former boss calls you up and says, "Bob, we've got a real doozy at the plant. I'd like you to come down and solve it for us."

You agree to help. But when you tackle the problem, you find that it takes an awfully long time to study the blueprint. You can't remember the specifications. You're unable to concentrate for more than a few minutes at a time. Your brain doesn't work the way it used to.

You tell your former boss you're sorry but you can't help him this time. But what if he calls again?

You have to do something.

YOUR DECISION

1. Admit you're getting old and get used to the idea that your brainpower is on the downgrade.

2. Start putting your brain to work and get it back into shape.

3. Figure something's wrong with you and go see a doctor.

HOW TO GET WHAT YOU WANT

Don't apply your middle-aged attitude: I don't have to do anything to keep my mind sharp. If it doesn't generate its usual brainpower, something must be medically wrong with me. Reject decision 3.

Do apply your emotionally mature retirement attitude: I must work at keeping my mind sharp.

Based on this new attitude, your emotionally mature retirement decision is

2. Start putting your brain to work and get it back into shape.

In middle age, your work kept your brain at work. Constant use kept your mental abilities sharp. You weren't aware of this. You took your brainpower for granted, like breathing. You didn't have to do anything to keep up your breathing level (unless you were sick), and you didn't have to do anything to keep up your brainpower level (unless you were sick).

But when you retire, you often retire your brain. It becomes like a motor that was left idle too long without use. When you call on it to perform, it sputters or doesn't turn over at all. Your brain doesn't wear out—it rusts out from lack of use.

When you accept your new emotionally mature attitude toward brainpower, you realize you've got to remove the rust so that the engine can run again.

How to do it? Easy. Learn a new skill. Do more reading. Swap opinions and argue points. Sign up for classes. Go to lectures. Get into discussion groups. Write letters to editors. Figure out puzzles. Think of ways of saving and making money (what an incentive that is to keeping your mind razor sharp!). Most important—get involved with the world again. (Making the right friends is one way to do it.)

This is an undisputed medical fact: If you keep on using your memory, your intelligence, and your powers of concentration (those three add up to your brainpower), you can preserve each of them and even boost their efficiency. That means no decrease in brainpower and possibly an increase. That's what you want in retirement from your brainpower.

Problem Area Number Six: Self-improvement

You want *the kind of self-improvement that makes you look better on the outside and feel better on the inside.*

YOUR SPECIFIC PROBLEM

You're a sixty-five-year-old retired salesperson. Recently you've had some difficult face-to-face encounters with your mirror. Every time you've looked into it, you've discovered a new wrinkle.

You ferret out a picture of yourself taken five years ago. You wonder why you didn't realize then how good you looked! You'd like to look that way again. You announce you're going to get a face-lifting.

Your spouse is against it. "I can understand," he or she says, "if you were still working and had to impress your customers. Or if you were looking for another mate. It makes no sense. You're just throwing your money away."

You have to do something.

YOUR DECISION

1. Agree with your spouse that a face-lifting makes sense only in middle age and cease and desist.
2. Go ahead with your face-lifting.
3. Outwit the aging clock by outfitting yourself with a wardrobe suitable for someone thirty or forty years younger.

HOW TO GET WHAT YOU WANT

Don't apply your middle-aged attitude: I improve myself to get ahead in sex and business.

Do apply your emotionally mature retirement attitude: I improve myself to please myself. Reject decision 1.

Based on this new attitude, your emotionally mature retirement decision is

2. Go ahead with your face-lifting.

Do anything else you wish to improve yourself, provided it pleases you. If it pleases you to see a younger face in the mirror, start shopping for a plastic surgeon today.

Do you have to have plastic surgery to improve yourself on the outside? Of course not. You can look better through good health, diet, the right clothes, exercise, and cosmetics. Keep your new attitude in mind and choose the way of self-improvement that pleases you. If you can feel better on the inside by doing some simple thing that *does* please you, like getting a new hairstyle or a new hairpiece, do it.

However, don't make the mistake of wearing young people's clothes even if it pleases you. This is not a form of self-improvement. You're simply masquerading as a young person. When you were a child, you dressed up in your parent's clothes. Now you dress up in your children's. There's a name for that behavior. It's called second childhood.

Looking better on the outside can make you feel better on the inside, and that's the kind of self-improvement you want in retirement.

Problem Area Number Seven: Image (the way younger people see you)

You want *a new image that younger people will respect (to replace the one you lost when you began to look old)*.

YOUR SPECIFIC PROBLEM

You're sixty-eight. You stop off for a hamburger. The counterman calls you Pop.

You have to do something.

YOUR DECISION

1. Change your image.
2. Get used to the idea that "Pop" is your new image and grin and bear it.
3. Complain to the manager.

HOW TO GET WHAT YOU WANT

Don't apply your middle-aged attitude: I'm me, a distinct individual. I have the right to be respected as one. Reject decision 3. (If you complain to the manager that you resent being called Pop, he may look at you in surprise and say, "Why, isn't every old man called Pop?" He's assumed you're like every other older man. In the eyes of many younger people, once you're older, you lose your individuality.)

Do apply your new emotionally mature retirement attitude: I have to work at being a distinct individual.

Based on this new attitude, your emotionally mature retirement decision is

1. Change your image.

When your children call you Pop, it's a term of affection. When a stranger calls you Pop, it's the same (whether or not it's intentional) as a racially degrading name. Racially degrading terms state loud and clear that all members of another race look alike, smell alike, act alike, and are in every way inferior. That's the ugliness of racism. In retirement, you may become the victim of a prejudice every bit as vicious as racism. It's called ageism.

With one apparently innocent word, *Pop*, the counterman turned you into a stereotype of a creaky old man—dull, seedy, and passive. This image is deeply ingrained in our society. Children, aged three through eleven, examined in a survey conducted by Duke University viewed the elderly as "sick," "sad," "tired," and "dirty." The children insisted they would never be old themselves.

Do you like that image? Then don't grin and bear it. Accept your new attitude: I must work at being a distinct individual. And do it. Here's how.

It's your appearance and manner that younger people see, your physical image. Don't let yourself run down. Keep your brain spinning; when you're mentally alert, any dull look you may have will vanish. Stay trim and keep your weight near the ideal for your age and height. Be fastidious about your clothes, and far from looking seedy, you'll look more attractive. (Many younger people believe there's an odor that comes with age. There isn't. But some older people do wear the same clothes for long periods of time without a trip to the cleaner's. Don't let clothes odor age you.) Speak up with authority, look people straight in the eye, and make it clear by the way you hold your head that you'll put up with no nonsense.

In short, refuse to conform to what ageists think you should look like, smell like, and act like. Break the stereotype. When you don't project the image of a Pop, they won't call you Pop. They'll see you as another human being like themselves—an individual in your own right and worthy of their respect. And that's the way you want younger people to see you; that's the new image you want in retirement.

6

How to Get What You Want from Life

In this chapter, you'll learn how to get what you want from your free time, your money, your food, your home, your hobby, your work (if you choose to work), your travel, and from your desire for safety—in short, from the situations and things that make up your life in retirement.

To do so, you must apply the remaining eight new emotionally mature retirement attitudes to problems in each of eight key retirement problem areas. Quiz yourself, as you did in the preceding chapter, to discover whether you're able to use these attitudes to make the right decisions to the following eight typical, tough problems.

Problem Area Number Eight: Free time

You want *pleasurable use of your free time.*

YOUR SPECIFIC PROBLEM

You've been retired for three years. All you've done in this time is wander around town (new buildings under construction fascinate you), read, go to the movies, and do whatever has struck your fancy at the moment. You've had a ball, and you're still having it. But there's a fly in the ointment—your friends tell you you're throwing your life away, and your spouse contemptuously calls you a sidewalk superintendent.

You have to do something.

YOUR DECISION

1. Do things to enjoy yourself that others may approve more of, like golfing, fishing, tennis, card playing, and so on.

2. Sign up for volunteer work.

3. Continue to do whatever you want to do, whenever you want to do it—even if it means doing nothing.

HOW TO GET WHAT YOU WANT

Don't apply your middle-aged attitude: I must fill up my free time in socially approved ways. Reject decision 1. (When free time in retirement becomes a hodgepodge of socially approved games, it's simply a continuation of the leisure life imposed on you in your middle years. If you're like many retirees who didn't like to play golf or bridge and who did it only because it was expected of them, now's the time to decline invitations gracefully.)

Do apply your emotionally mature retirement attitude: I can do anything I want with my free time, including nothing, as long as it gives me pleasure.

Based on this new attitude, your emotionally mature retirement decision is

3. Continue to do whatever you want to do, whenever you want to do it—even if it means doing nothing.

Work can be a most satisfactory way of filling your

free time. But organized volunteer work for older people is often make-work: paper shuffling, purposeless meetings and phone calls, and unnecessary errands. It often bears the same relationship to real work as diet food bears to real food—attractive and easy to swallow but potentially unsatisfying. The "organized volunteer" ends up not only empty-handed but also empty of the emotional satisfaction that doing a real job provides. "You'll never get me sealing envelopes to promote a cookie sale," grimly announces a retired doctor.

And he doesn't have to. Neither do you. Just follow your new attitude and you can do anything you want to do. If you choose to lick stamps without pay, that's your business. If you choose to play golf, that's up to you. And if you choose not to do a blessed thing, you have the right to not do it. There's just one proviso—whatever you do, it has to please you. That's how to get the pleasurable use of your free time in retirement.

Problem Area Number Nine: Money

You want *a way to get the most out of your shrunken money supply.*

YOUR SPECIFIC PROBLEM

You've just bought three dresses for a trip you're planning to make. The total cost is $475. Your retired husband is shocked. He says, "Look, we're dipping into our savings. I'm afraid of inflation. I think we'll live to a hundred, and I want our money to last. I want some money left over to leave to the kids. So from now on, I'm setting up a budget—and we're going to stick to it."

You have to do something.

YOUR DECISION

1. Refuse to go on a budget, but volunteer to restrict your spending.
2. Agree to a budget and promise to stick to it.
3. Tell him you won't go on a budget because you want to be able to buy the things you see advertised—things that your friends have.

HOW TO GET WHAT YOU WANT

Don't apply your middle-aged attitude: I need money to keep up with the Joneses. Reject decision 3.

Do apply your emotionally mature retirement attitude: I use the money left after we've paid our basic bills to buy only the things we need to make us happy.

Based on this new attitude, your emotionally mature decision is

1. Refuse to go on a budget, but volunteer to restrict your spending.

A woman who faced this problem tells why she came to this decision. "Retirement is a time of freedom. I don't like to be told, 'Do this. Do that. Stand here. Go there.' A budget restricts me. I hate that feeling. It's like being in a subway during the rush hour. I can't wait until I get out.

"But everything my husband says about money is true. I just never realized it before. While he was still working, I kept thinking, 'It's there to spend, and we can always get more.' But we can't now, can we? The well's run dry. We've got to make do and do without. Oh, that doesn't mean I'm going to turn into a skinflint. I've seen that happen to old people, and that dries them up. No, I'm just going to be prudent and sensible. Pay our bills for rent, groceries, and utilities—you know, the necessities. And we'll spend what's left over on what we need to make us happy. Only what we need—no more, no less. One long-distance call will do; why make it two? One dress will do, why buy three?"

She returned two of the three dresses.

And when you use your surplus cash to buy only the things that make you happy (you'll be surprised how little that is when you're not keeping up with the Joneses), you don't need a formal budget; you're automatically budget-wise. Your new attitude is actually a way to get the most out of your shrunken money supply. In addition, you retain your precious retirement freedom.

Problem Area Number Ten: Food

You want *the kind of food that's best for you.*

YOUR SPECIFIC PROBLEM

Your wife has become a vegetarian. Her typical dinner consists of a baked potato, steamed peas, a salad, and cheese. You're a steak eater. She won't cook for you because the sight of meat makes her nauseated. When you grill a steak for yourself, she won't eat with you. She seems to glow with well-being, but you're miserable.

You have to do something.

YOUR DECISION

1. Eat your meals out, even though it may strain your budget.

2. Become a vegetarian yourself (well, a good part of the time).

3. Feel that you can eat whatever tastes good to you and insist that she eat with you.

HOW TO GET WHAT YOU WANT

Don't apply your middle-aged attitude: Food must taste good. (That's why you ate so much junk food, even though you knew better.) Reject decision 3.

Do apply your emotionally mature retirement attitude: Food must give me a sense of well-being in addition to supplying my nutritional needs.

Based on this new attitude, your emotionally mature decision is

> 2. Become a vegetarian yourself (well, a good part of the time).

Go over the facts in this problem, and you'll find that one stands out—her sense of well-being. She is no longer asking, "What tastes good?" or even "What's good for me?" She chooses her food on the basis of "what makes me *feel* good?" It is an *emotional* choice. It has come about this way.

Like so many older people, she felt her body sending out its not-so-subtle signals of decline. But she wouldn't let herself feel less than great. She believed a vegetable diet would make her feel great, and it did. That's not to say vegetarianism is the cure-all its adherents claim it to be. It may be and it may not. But that's not the point. The point is, it gave her the emotional uplift she needed to survive one of the critical tests of oncoming age. It made her feel on top of the world despite her aches and pains.

It's quite likely that any other prudent diet with a sound nutritional base would have produced the same result. But *her* diet is the one you're stuck with. If it produces a sense of well-being in her, isn't it likely to produce a sense of well-being in you? Let your new attitude be your guide, and try it. (You don't have to be a fanatic about it. Whenever the moon is full, and an irresistible urge comes over you to sink your teeth into red meat, lope to your nearest steak house.)

Chances are, you'll feel as wonderful as she does—on a diet, fortunately, that's packed with the nutrients you need. That's the best kind of food for you—and that's what you want in retirement.

The bonus is that you and your wife will sit down at the same table together. Sharing food is one of the most intimate of human acts. It is a time of warmth and communication. It brings you closer together. And isn't that better than chomping on a steak in some restaurant, alone?

Problem Area Number Eleven: Home

You want *a home that meets your retirement needs without restricting your freedom.*

YOUR SPECIFIC PROBLEM

Your spouse wants to move to a retirement community. He or she reasons, "In a retirement community, we can get everything we want to make us happy in old age."

You object. You reason, "In a retirement community, I can't always do what I want to do when I want to do it."

You're deadlocked.

You have to do something.

YOUR DECISION

1. Agree to move to a retirement community at the sacrifice of your personal freedom.

2. Find close to home all (or most of) the facilities that your spouse feels a retirement community offers.

3. Refuse to make any move; if your home was good enough to bring up your children in, it's good enough for you now.

HOW TO GET WHAT YOU WANT

Don't apply your middle-aged attitude: My home is something special because it's a place for my children. Reject decision 3. (Your children now have homes of their own. Sentiment is a sweet emotion, but it can block the solution to your retirement problems.)

Do apply your emotionally mature retirement attitude: My home is something special because it's a place from which I can easily reach my retirement activities whenever I choose.

Based on this attitude, your emotionally mature decision is

2. Find close to home all (or most of) the facilities that your spouse feels a retirement community offers.

Is carrying out this decision a tall order? Not really. Listen in on this taped conversation between a husband and wife who faced this problem. She had suggested that instead of moving to a retirement community, they take an apartment ("It'll save money, too") in the Oakland section of Pittsburgh.

HE: That's ridiculous.
SHE: No, it's not. You can have everything there that you'd want in a retirement community.
HE: I don't see it at all.
SHE: All right. What specifically do you want in a retirement community?
HE: One by one?
SHE: Yes, one by one.
HE: I want to go swimming, get exercise.
SHE: There's a health club four blocks away.
HE: I want to play golf.
SHE: There's a golf course five minutes away.
HE: I'd like to take long walks where there are trees and grass.

SHE: The University of Pittsburgh campus is across the street. It's a beautiful place to walk through.
HE: What about crafts and things? I've always wanted to learn.
SHE: How many schools do you think there are in Pittsburgh teaching just that? Dozens! And don't tell me you're going to a retirement community for entertainment. One night a week? A second-run movie? There are theaters of every type in Pittsburgh, only minutes away. Films. Ballet. Drama. And art galleries, museums, and libraries. Enough entertainment for you?
HE: I concede all this. But I want to make friends.
SHE: You think you'll make them in a retirement community? Maybe. But you'll also be pretty close to people you don't like. Why not be sure to meet people with the same interests? You're going to a health club, to craft classes—you'll meet them there. You're interested in public affairs. We'll go to lectures. You'll meet them there. Make an effort, anywhere, to meet people, and you will—all kinds of people.
HE: Makes sense.
SHE: Know what's wrong with you?
HE: No.
SHE: You think retirement is a time to let down, to let other people do for you.
HE: It's not?
SHE: No, it's not. It's a time to do for yourself— more than ever before. Don't let yourself down.

He agreed to the apartment. At first she worked up a weekly schedule of activities and made all the arrangements. After a while he began doing it himself. He liked that better.

Guided by her emotionally mature attitude, this understanding woman provided virtually all the benefits of a retirement community without the loss of his freedom or hers—close to their home. And isn't that what you want from your home in retirement?

You don't have to move, however, to make your home a center of retirement activities. Look around and you may find all or a good many of the things you want to do not too far from your own backyard.

Problem Area Number Twelve: Hobby

You want *a hobby that's right for you in retirement.*

YOUR SPECIFIC PROBLEM

You've been a very active woman all your adult life. You've managed a big-city boutique. At sixty-five, you retire and go and live with your bachelor son in his home in the country. You've never learned to cook, so you can't help out in the kitchen. A woman comes in to clean and shop. There's nothing for you to do, and you feel your life is empty.

Your son suggests you take up a hobby. You tell him, "I had a hobby once when I was working—photography. It was great for relaxing when I was under stress. But I'm not under stress now. Just the reverse—I have no stress at all in my life. So what good's a hobby?"

You have to do something.

YOUR DECISION

1. Accept the fact that there's no hobby right for you in retirement and learn to live with boredom.
2. Take another whack at photography.

3. Look for a hobby that doesn't relax you but instead stimulates you.

HOW TO GET WHAT YOU WANT

Don't apply your middle-aged attitude: I need a hobby to relax me under stress. Reject decision 2.

Do apply your emotionally mature retirement attitude: I need a hobby to provide satisfaction with life.

Based on this new attitude, your emotionally mature decision is

3. Look for a hobby that doesn't relax you but instead stimulates you.

I ask preretirees, "What are you going to do when you retire?"

Eight out of ten respond, "I'll have a chance to devote my time to my hobbies." They say it with a gleam of anticipation in their eyes. But too often that gleam turns into a dull stare.

The hobbies you had in your middle years were escapes from the frenetic pace of work and the pressures of bringing up a family. They were nondrug sedatives. But in retirement, life itself can become a sedative. If your old hobbies do not adequately stimulate you, putting more time into them may act like an overdose. Working at your hobbies may become a dreary mechanical task performed in a kind of torpor.

There may not be much joy in going fishing to get away from it all when there's nothing to get away from. Your joy sours to apathy. Unless your middle-aged hobby was a passion, it may be a dud in retirement.

What you need in retirement may be the reverse of what you looked for before—an explosive hobby that excites you, stimulates you, and gives you an interest in life. What kind of hobby can do that?

That's for you to decide. What makes another person's skin crawl can make yours tingle. A middle-aged hobby that's boring the retiree down the block to tears can be your cup of tea. Try on different hobbies much as you'd try on items of clothing—until you find the one that makes you come alive. Hobby shopping in itself is an invigorating hobby.

The right hobby triggers a chain reaction that gets you going again. You find your pleasure in life returning. Your morale improves. You take an interest in everything around you. You're more alert and eager to make friends. You plunge into things. Your hobby, in itself and in what it does for you, gives you a sense of satisfaction in life.

That kind of hobby is right for you and is the kind of hobby you want in retirement.

Satisfaction in life has so beneficial an effect on your health that according to researchers at the Gerontology Research Center, affiliated with the University of Maryland at College Park, it can lengthen your life span five to ten years.

Problem Area Number Thirteen: Work

You want *the kind of job you need in retirement if you decide to go back to work*.

YOUR SPECIFIC PROBLEM

You're a recently retired accountant and financially secure. You're offered a consultant spot with your old firm at $150 a day, one day a week. You're also offered a job at a local business school teaching accounting. The pay there is $125 a week, four nights a week.

You never were crazy about working as an accountant. You never disliked it, either. You just did it. But as a young man, you taught accounting briefly, and you've never forgotten what a kick you got out of it. You've always dreamed of being able to return to teaching.

But you compare incomes—$150 a week as a consultant with $125 a week as a teacher—and you figure you'd lose $1,300 a year if you take the teaching job. That's a lot of money in retirement, even if you are financially secure.

You have to do something.

YOUR DECISION

1. Take the consultant job.
2. Take the teaching job.
3. Decide that retirement is a time for fun and take neither.

HOW TO GET WHAT YOU WANT

Don't apply your middle-aged attitude: I need the work because I need the money. If I get job satisfaction thrown in, that's fine, but I'm used to getting along without it. Reject decision 1.

Do apply your emotionally mature retirement attitude: If I can live on my retirement income, I need work that gives me job satisfaction. If I can't, I need work that earns money, whether it gives me job satisfaction or not.

Based on this attitude, your emotionally mature retirement decision is

2. Take the teaching job.

If you don't need money in retirement and you have a choice between a job that gives you satisfaction and one that doesn't, take the job that gives you a glow. But, realistically, you might not have much of a choice. Take a look at these dismal facts.

There are millions of older Americans able and willing to work, but there are virtually no jobs available to them. Private enterprise, with a handful of exceptions, has turned its back on its retirees, and of its $450 billion budget for jobs, the federal government sets aside only a tiny fraction for jobs for retirees. What few jobs are available from Uncle Sam pay poorly, some as little as thirty-two dollars a week for Foster Grandparents. Inadequate income in retirement, because of restricted employment opportunities, is the number-one problem affecting a substantial number of older Americans, according to the Senate's Special Committee on Aging.

If you need the money, you should take the job you can get and hang the job satisfaction. Your new retirement attitude says, "Go ahead and do it. It's the right thing to do." With that attitude, even though you're settling for something less than ideal, you'll feel no emotional pain.

A great many people enter retirement with sufficient savings and investments to free them from financial pressures. If you're among this section of retirees, you have the opportunity to look for a job that will give you the satisfaction you need for your happiness.

You may not have been able to do that in middle age. If you're like many of the present generation of retirees, you might have spent your working life at something you really didn't want to do. You might have changed jobs, but you almost never changed your line of work. With a family to support, you couldn't afford the time and money to train for a new career. The doors of opportunity were shut to you. You continued to do at the end of your working life what you began doing at its onset, never having a chance to try something else, something you could look forward to every morning.

In retirement, you have that chance. Let your new attitude guide you.

Look for a job that gives you emotional satisfaction, that is, gives you a kick out of the actual work you do. That's what job satisfaction is all about. If you know that a job you like is available but you need training to get it, go back to school. Nothing's stopping you. Besides, working toward your goal is often as rewarding as reaching it. And if you're fortunate and have a choice of jobs, pick the one that gives you the most job satisfaction, even if it pays less. And if you're very fortunate, you may land a job that gives you both job satisfaction and money. Many consultant jobs for which you're qualified do just that, and so do most of the jobs you give yourself when you're self-employed.

So, if you decide to get a job, rely on your new attitude toward work to direct you to the kind of job you need —a job that provides money, a job that provides job satisfaction, or, ideally, a job that provides both. That's what you want when you go back to work in retirement.

You should take note of the following: If you can live on your retirement income and do not need to supplement it, you have the option to work or not to work. If doing nothing makes you happy, do nothing. But if doing nothing doesn't make you happy, not working can present a serious health hazard. The American Medical Association has said that "sudden cessation of productive work and earning power due to retirement often leads to physical and emotional deterioration and premature death." Don't be taken in by the myth that retirement life should be all fun and games. Give up your unhappy canasta sessions and look for a job. It could lengthen your life.

Problem Area Number Fourteen: Travel

You want to travel in order to break out of your retirement shell.

YOUR SPECIFIC PROBLEM

You've moved into your retirement home. The weather is in the balmy seventies all year long. Behind you is a 200-acre pond where, on the spur of the moment, you can boat, fish, or swim. A few miles away are the waters of the Pacific, where surf-fishing is challenging and productive. You bicycle, hike, dine out, and explore the woodlands and gentle wildlife around you. You laze in the sun.

Your wife joins you in your activities. She seems to enjoy them as much as you do. But there's a flaw in her contentment. One day, as you're snoozing in your hammock, she plunks a folder of travel brochures on your chest. "Wake up!" she cries. "Retirement is travel time!" You point out you're already on vacation—a permanent one; there's no need to travel. She doesn't buy it.

You have to do something.

YOUR DECISION

1. Please her and sign up for the same kind of vacation you went on before retirement.

2. Agree to take trips with a purpose other than just having fun tourist style.

3. Make it clear to her that she's living out every retiree's dream and don't budge.

HOW TO GET WHAT YOU WANT

Don't apply your middle-aged attitude: I need to travel to escape from the pressures of the world. Reject decision 1.

Do apply your emotionally mature retirement attitude: I need to travel to get back into the world, without pressure (in addition to having a wonderful time).

Based on this new attitude, your emotionally mature retirement decision is

2. Agree to take trips with a purpose other than just having fun tourist style.

Too often, your retirement wonderland is a shell. It's a luxurious hermitage separated from the active world. The first few years are marvelous. You believe you'll never tire of the contrast between the harsh, clamorous, and pressuring world you left behind and the beautifully serene world in which you live. But you do tire. The sameness, the isolation, and the removal from challenges open the way to the affluent retiree's greatest enemy—boredom.

You've got to break out of your shell. Travel can do it for you.

Follow your new emotional attitude. Use travel to get you involved with the world again—this time without pressure. Get involved with people, renew old friendships, and make new ones. Attend conventions, meetings, and seminars. Go wherever things that interest you are happening. Go wherever things are happening period; you may find many new things there to interest you. Leisurely take in the world's art shows, theaters, and museums. Traveling this way makes you feel part of things, and that's a wonderful souvenir to take home with you.

You don't have to be affluent to travel to widen your horizons. Travel in retirement can be a journey to find your roots a continent away, or it can be a bus ride to a nearby organic farm. It can throw your mind open to exotic architecture, food, languages, and peoples, or it can introduce you to an artisan in the next village. It can be a ride on a yak or on Amtrak. It doesn't matter what it costs or where you go, provided that at the end of the journey, you've broken out of your retirement shell. And that's what you want from travel in retirement.

Problem Area Number Fifteen: Safety

You want *a maximum of safety with a minimum of fear.*

YOUR SPECIFIC PROBLEM

You're at home all day in a large house with only your spouse to "protect" you. You become obsessed with the fear of muggings, burglary, arson, and even murder. When you meet friends, no matter what the topic of conversation is, you always manage to work in horror stories about what happened to people like yourself and your spouse. You invariably conclude with, "What I'm afraid of is it could happen to us, too."

One day a friend takes you aside. "Look," he says, "I hate to tell you this, but you've become a 'safety bore.' All your friends are sick and tired of hearing you whine and complain all the time. When we see you coming down the street, we cross over to the other side."

You have to do something.

YOUR DECISION

1. Move to a retirement community employing a twenty-four-hour security force.
2. Invest in a reasonable amount of sophisticated anticrime equipment for your home.
3. Realize that violence and crime, especially against the old, is a spreading social disease, and learn to live with it as you do many of the other destructive forces of modern life.

HOW TO GET WHAT YOU WANT

Do apply your middle-aged attitude: I must do everything I can to provide for my family's safety and my own.

Your attitude in retirement is the same except for two things. It's just you and your spouse you're worried about, and because both of you are more vulnerable to attack than in middle age, your desire to do everything to protect yourself is more intense now than it was then.

Reject decision 3. It's self-defeating and self-degrading to accept a passive role as an inevitable victim.

Based on your emotionally mature retirement attitude, your decision is either

    1. Move to a retirement community employing a twenty-four-hour security force,

    or, if you can't stand the restrictions of that kind of life,

    2. Invest in a reasonable amount of sophisticated anticrime equipment for your home, such as electronic locks, alarm systems, TV monitors, and so on. And if you're fond of animals, add an old-fashioned unsophisticated crime fighter—a dog whose bite is worse than its bark.

Either decision gives you a maximum of safety with a minimum of fear in retirement.

Now you know the emotionally mature retirement attitudes that give you the ability to solve your problems in the fifteen key retirement problem areas.

Does that mean you're equipped to lead a happy life in retirement?

You are not—yet.

You still have other retirement problems to solve.

   · How can you get along with younger people?

   · How can you further break the silence barrier that springs up between you and your spouse during retirement?

   · How can you deal with your fear of death?

   · How can you avoid loneliness, particularly after the death of your spouse?

   · How can you enjoy sex as you get older?

- How can you fight the emotional blackmail used against older people?

- How can you prevent or cure the shock of mandatory retirement?

- How can you choose between living in a retirement community and living in the real world?

- How can you gain the respect and admiration of your community—even though it may be hostile to older people?

And, finally,

- How can you transform the emotional losses of old age, the most devastating losses you can suffer in the normal course of your life, into emotional triumphs?

These are problems that have just begun to surface in the scientific study of aging. That's why they have not yet been included in any list of key retirement problems. But these problems are as important, if not far more important, to your happiness and to your health as any problem you'll encounter in the standard fifteen key retirement problem areas.

7

How to Communicate with Younger People

Mary Lindsay is a retired telephone operator. She has excellent typing skills and has always wanted to work as a typist. She qualified for the roster of a temporary personnel service. This type of service hires individuals and rents them out to businesses needing their help for a part of a day, a full day, or a week or longer. Mary found she could choose the companies she worked for and even choose the locations and the hours. This could have been a dream come true except for one thing—at almost every company Mary worked, the regular typists were hostile to her.

Mary's case is not unique. Many men and women going back to work during retirement experience from younger workers displays of antagonism ranging from slight snubs to such mild sabotage as "Sorry, I just don't know where that file is. You'll just have to hunt for it yourself."

The reason? "It's because we're older," the working retirees sadly conclude. But the hostility of younger workers has nothing to do with age as such.

Why are younger people often hostile to retirees?

If Mary Lindsay had asked the younger typists why they didn't like her, they would have answered, "You work too hard." "You're a perfectionist." "You never complain." "You always say yes to overtime." "You never goof off." "You make us look bad by comparison." Most of them would have admitted they thought Mary was after their job. Of course, she wasn't. The thought of taking a permanent job never crossed her mind. How had this misunderstanding come about?

In the most common way possible. The younger people had one attitude toward work, and it never occurred to them that Mary could have another. But Mary did. It was, I want work that gives me job satisfaction, and I can get that satisfaction only when I give my job my all. But the attitude of the younger typists might have been, I want to work only to make money. Or, the less I do, the more I can get away with, and the sooner I get out of the office, the better I'll feel. Or, this job is just a stepping-stone to a better one. The attitudes were on a collision course, and it was Mary who was the emotional victim of the crash.

The hostility of younger people to retirees often arises from a clash of attitudes.

How can you prevent hostility from younger people caused by conflicting attitudes?

To stifle the hostility of the younger typists before it had a chance to surface, Mary Lindsay could have said,

"Look, I'm working the way I do because it's the only way I can get a kick out of it. I don't want your job—I like temporary jobs. But if you have some overloads I can take off your desk to make your work easier, I'd enjoy doing it."

When you explain your attitudes to younger people, you can nip their hostility in the bud.

How can you explain your attitudes to younger people?

You must start by having a sharp picture in your mind of just what your attitudes are.

I'm referring, of course, to emotionally mature retirement attitudes. These are the attitudes that have changed so radically from those of your middle years (with the exception of your attitude on safety). It is because of these changes that an explanation is in order to those younger people who live by the middle-aged attitudes that you have discarded.

You know what your new attitudes should be. You saw them solve difficult retirement problems for you (see chapters 5 and 6) that got you what you wanted from yourself and other people and from the things and situations that make up your retirement life. But have you adopted these attitudes and really made them part of your life? Find out by using the following checklist.

The checklist gives you a choice of an emotionally mature middle-aged attitude or an emotionally mature retirement attitude for the standard fifteen key retirement problem areas. Just check off the attitudes you now hold. The first part of the checklist helps you review your attitudes toward yourself and other people; the second, toward situations and things. Now, find your attitudes.

WHAT ARE YOUR RETIREMENT ATTITUDES?

Select either A or B for each key retirement problem area.

Key Retirement Problem Areas	Your Attitudes A	B
Number One Children	My children come first at all times and at all costs.	My spouse and I come first, but I'll do as much as I can in an emergency without jeopardizing our happiness.
Number Two Marriage	I share as many nonwork activities with my spouse as possible.	My spouse and I are both individuals with the right to do our own thing without interference from each other.
Number Three Friends	The right friends for me are couples in my age group, with whom I share my social life.	My friends can be of any age or sex as long as I can share my intimate thoughts and emotions with them and rely on them to be my channels to the outside world, that of nonretirement activities.

Key Retirement Problem Areas	Your Attitudes A	B
Number Four Health	The chance of any serious illness striking me or my spouse is small.	Serious illness can strike anytime, and I will care for my afflicted spouse if it does.
Number Five Brainpower	I don't have to do anything to keep my mind sharp. If it doesn't generate its usual brainpower, something must be medically wrong with me.	I must work at keeping my mind sharp.
Number Six Self-Improvement	I improve myself to get ahead in sex and business.	I improve myself to please myself.
Number Seven Image (the way younger people see you)	I'm me, a distinct individual. I have the right to be respected as one.	I have to work at being a distinct individual.

Key Retirement Problem Areas	Your Attitudes A	B
Number Eight Free Time	I must fill up my free time in socially approved ways.	I can do anything I want with my free time, including nothing—as long as what I do gives me pleasure.
Number Nine Money	I need money to keep up with the Joneses.	I use the money left after I've paid our basic bills to buy only the things I need to make me happy.
Number Ten Food	Food must taste good.	Food must give me a sense of well-being (in addition to supplying my nutritional needs).
Number Eleven Home	My home is something special because it's a place for my children.	My home is something special because it's a place from which I can easily reach retirement activities whenever I choose to do so.
Number Twelve Hobby	I need a hobby to relax me under stress.	I need a hobby to provide satisfaction in life.

Key Retirement Problem Areas	Your Attitudes A	B
Number Thirteen Work	I need to work because I need the money. If I get job satisfaction thrown in, that's fine; but I'm used to getting along without it.	If I can live on my retirement income, I need work that gives me job satisfaction. If I can't, I need work that earns me money, whether it gives me job satisfaction or not.
Number Fourteen Travel	I need to travel to escape from the pressures of my world.	I need to travel to get back into the world, without pressure (in addition to having a wonderful time).
Number Fifteen Safety	I must do everything I can to provide for my family's safety and my own.	I must do everything I can to provide for my spouse's safety and my own. But because we're more vulnerable, my desire to protect ourselves is more intense than it was in middle age.

You've recognized that checks in the A column identify the emotionally mature middle-aged attitudes you still hold. Checks in the B column identify your emotionally mature attitudes in retirement.

If you still cling to a few middle-aged attitudes, don't be upset. It's not unusual for retirees to find their attitudes are emotionally mature in some key retirement problem areas and emotionally immature in others. Many retirees, for example, are emotionally mature about money but emotionally immature about their children. You may wish to go back and review the four guidelines in chapters 2, 3, and 4.

Now that you know what decisions are right for you, you can make them without (or with less) guilt. For example, when you know your new attitude toward your children should be "My spouse and I come first," if your children ask you for money that they could earn for themselves with a little effort, you shouldn't question for a second your decision to say no, and you shouldn't feel a twinge of guilt.

You know what your emotionally mature retirement attitudes are. What do you do next to make them clear to younger people?

Look up any of your fifteen key retirement attitudes in the checklist on the preceding pages and put the description you find there into your own words. Here's a typical example.

Your middle-aged neighbor invites you to her home on her card night. She tells you you're welcome to bring some friends along. You tell her most of your friends don't play cards.

"You mean to tell me your friends don't play cards!" she exclaims in astonishment. The tone in her voice adds,

"What kind of freak are you to have friends like that?"

There's nothing like being different to create instant hostility. So you have to act fast. You do. You have a clear-cut picture of your attitude toward friends because you've studied the checklist.

You spin off, "Some of my best friends do play cards. And I enjoy a game myself from time to time. But I don't pick my friends just because they play cards. I'm getting older, and I have more time to spend with my friends. We can really get to know one another, which is a lot of comfort as a person gets on in years. Besides, I'm out of things in retirement, and my friends are active and interesting, and they kind of get me back into things.

"You see, a retired person has special problems and special ways to solve them. I hope you understand."

She will. Anybody would.

How wide is the understanding gap between you and middle-aged people?

As wide as it could possibly be. It's up to you to close it. You can understand their attitudes (you've lived through them), but they can't understand yours until you make them understand.

Your children are middle-aged. Does that mean there is an enormous understanding gap between you and them?

Yes. Perhaps even wider than between you and other middle-agers. That's because your children are closer to you; they see your new attitudes taking over, and they may be alienated by them. An emotionally mature retiree may be accused by a child in words like these: "You've changed. You don't love me anymore."

Answer that with, "Yes, I have changed. I'm proud of it. I'm being the person I've always wanted to be. I have to think of what's good for me.

"But not love you anymore? That's silly. I love you more. But I don't love you as an infant or a child. I love you as an adult, as an individual. But not as any individual—as a special one, my flesh and blood. And I hope you'll love me the same way."

Explain your new attitudes to your children just as you would explain them to any other middle-aged person. They'll see you in a new light, a far more endearing one.

You see, when you retain the attitudes of your middle age, your attitudes will match those of your children, and there's no understanding gap. But you'll be in trouble. For example, you may treat them as children at a time in their lives when they'd prefer (in most cases) to be treated like the adults they are.

Many retirees retain their middle-aged attitudes. Is there an understanding gap between you and them?

Yes. It's the same gap you'll find between you and a middle-ager.

That's why many emotionally mature retirees shun retirement communities. The members of a retirement community are likely to cling to middle-aged attitudes that call for a socially approved and organized life. It would be unrealistic to expect these retirees to understand the new retirement attitudes based on freedom and individuality no matter how lucidly and forcefully they're explained. Emotionally mature retirees find the understanding gap between them and members of a retirement community difficult to bridge. (See chapter 14 for more on retirement communities.)

Is communicating with young adults more difficult than communicating with middle-agers?

Oftentimes, no. Your emotionally mature attitudes have much in common with some of the more liberated views of many of today's young people. Compare.

· These young people feel their mates have the right to do their own thing. So do you.

· They select friends who satisfy them emotionally and open new vistas to them. So do you.

· They improve themselves to please themselves. So do you.

· They use their time to do anything—or nothing. So do you.

· They disdain to use their money to keep up with the Joneses. So do you.

· They have a new respect for food—it must give them a sense of well-being as well as being nutritious. So do you.

· They regard their home as a center of activities. So do you.

· They are likely to work only at jobs that give them a sense of satisfaction. So do you (when you can afford it).

· They travel to get themselves involved with the world through contacts with new people, new ideas, and new cultures. So do you.

And, most of all,

· Many young people work at becoming distinct individuals. And so do you.

You and many of the nation's youth are on the same beam.

That's why emotionally mature retirees frequently get along better with their young-adult grandchildren than they do with their middle-aged children. I've known young people who after meeting emotionally mature retirees for the first time come away with comments like, "I never expected they'd be like that. They're super!" You and many young people have so many attitudes in common that they'll listen respectfully when you explain your attitudes that differ.

But there's one area in which the young can find no emotional rapport with the old. It's health. A person in his or her twenties can understand the inevitability of the body's decline with the head but never with the heart. So don't be a health bore. As a wise retiree, don't elaborate on your personal aches and pains when you're with young adults.

Caution: There are some adults who rush from their teens right into middle age. These young fogies don't like the attitudes of their liberated peers, and they won't like yours. If you feel it's necessary to make friends with that kind of person, explain your attitudes and in time you may be able to win him or her over.

Is explaining attitudes communication?

It's the vital part of communication.

What's communication, anyway?

First, here's what it's not.

It's not just talking. We live in a society that has the mistaken notion that if you just talk, everything will be all right. But you can talk until you're blue in the face, and if the other person doesn't understand your attitudes, you may as well be talking in Hindustani.

You don't always communicate with words. Actions speak louder and clearer if you know how to listen to them. And you know how when you understand the attitudes behind them.

Communication is the art of being understood by another person and of understanding that person.

How does explaining your attitudes to younger people and understanding their attitudes help you communicate with them?

Look at it this way: Younger people can misunderstand your opinions and actions. You can misunderstand theirs. But since opinions and actions are determined by a person's attitudes, when you understand a younger person's attitudes, you cannot misunderstand his or her opinions and actions. And your opinions and actions cannot be misunderstood when your attitudes are understood. Each of you understands what the other person says and does, and that's communication.

You understand younger people's attitudes, and you can explain yours to them. What else can you do to strengthen communication?

A great deal. If you're like many retirees, you have a mistaken idea that age grants you certain privileges as well as puts you at certain disadvantages when you talk to younger people. (I am including both young adults and middle-aged people.) Exploiting these privileges and letting the disadvantages cramp your style could become habits that wreck communication. Here's how to squelch the ten most destructive of these habits and replace them with habits that promote conversation, understanding, and even friendship.

GUIDELINES FOR BETTER COMMUNICATION WITH YOUNGER PEOPLE
---

1. *Don't* ho-hum their experiences because you've "gone all through it." *Do* show an interest in what they do and what's done to them. If you're interested in them, they'll be interested in you.

2. *Don't* think that because of your age, you have to act stiff and formal. You'll just freeze the conversation. *Do* act your age; that means being alert and animated and projecting your personality with warmth and friendliness.

3. *Don't* try to impress younger people with your "years of experience." *Do* call attention to a recent achievement of the younger person. He or she will regard that as a compliment.

4. *Don't* harp on "the good old days." They probably weren't as good as you'd like to think, and, besides, it could be a bore to people who didn't live through them. *Do* talk in the present tense.

5. *Don't* monopolize a conversation because you

feel younger people should "listen to their elders." *Do* let them express themselves on a give-and-take basis.

6. *Don't* talk about your retirement problems. Most younger people can't possibly understand them. *Do* let them talk about *their* problems. That's something you can understand, and you can listen with a sympathetic ear. They'll like that.

7. *Don't* think you can afford to be critical because you've "seen it all" and have better standards of comparison. You'll offend the younger person and dry up the conversation. (Do you like criticism?) *Do* find some good things to say about the person you're talking with and say them in a naturally friendly manner. It could be the start of a warm relationship.

8. *Don't* feel that a general conversation with a younger person is pointless because you've lost touch with things. When a younger person opens up a conversation of this type, you'll be likely to answer in terse noncommittal sentences that will mark you as dull. *Do* keep up a conversation. Keep up your interest in the world around you, which will help you contribute to discussion. You'll find yourself chatting smoothly and easily, and soon you'll be talking about things of personal interest to both of you.

9. *Don't* be timid about expressing yourself because you're afraid of the younger person's disapproval. You have a perfect right to think the way you do. Youth doesn't have a monopoly on correct answers. *Do* speak up. When you express your beliefs strongly and reasonably, you'll gain respect. The conversation can proceed with each of you learning from the other.

And, above all,

10. *Don't* give advice unless it's requested. Advice that's not asked for is seldom welcome, and those who need it most like it least. *Do* put your experience and knowledge on the line unstintingly whenever a younger person asks for it. That could be the most valuable form of help you can give.

Communication, as you have seen, is the art of getting along harmoniously with another person through mutual understanding. In retirement, there is one person in your life more important than any other—your spouse. In the next chapter, I'll show you how to communicate with your spouse to create a marriage more fulfilling, more rewarding, and happier than you had before. And you'll be doing this at a time of your life when communication in many marriages breaks down.

8

How to Make Your Marriage Better Than Before

The divorce rate among retirees is higher than among any other age group. And according to estimates from many retirement counselors, seven out of ten retired couples who do not divorce live in an atmosphere of mutual hostility. The shocking suicide rate among retirees, now climbing to unprecedented heights, is often ascribed to the heartbreak of unhappy marriages.

According to psychologist James J. Lynch, without love and companionship between husband and wife, millions of Americans are prone to virtually every major disease from mental illness to cancer. The unhappy spouse is a leading candidate for a heart attack. "We must learn to live together," warns Dr. Lynch, "or face the possibility of prematurely dying alone."

Why do many marriages go wrong in retirement?

The surface answer is emotional immaturity for retirement. But let's probe deeper and find out exactly how it works to wreck your marriage.

To be emotionally immature in retirement means that you're clinging to your middle-aged way of life. That way of life gave you and your spouse many things to talk about. There was your work, the kids, and the schools. There were your friends to be discussed, your home to be renovated, and the new car to be financed. There was subject matter for endless discussions.

But in retirement, that way of life has gone. If you're emotionally immature, no new way of life has moved in to take its place. There's nothing to talk about. You and your spouse are separated by a barrier of silence.

That doesn't mean that you don't talk to each other. But it's hollow talk, echoes of the conversations of years gone by. "Month after month, then day after day . . . one set of reminiscences, one choir of childish off-key opinions, habits, 'hopes and fears' . . . the same arguments and crises . . . the same gray spiritual landscape and foggy climate," writes Dr. William Gass, author of *On Being Blue*. Your spiritless exchanges are without significance. It's the same as if you had never spoken.

Sometimes, in an effort to say something, just anything, to your spouse, you babble about what you read in the newspapers or watch on TV. "Why don't you talk to me anymore?" a wife pleads with her retired husband. "But I do talk to you," he responds. "I talk politics." "That means you don't care about me anymore," she weeps. And she's right. He isn't talking to touch her heart. He might as well say nothing at all. (Through my research, I have found that it is mainly the men who put up the barrier of silence.)

Too often, a retiree simply stops talking about anything except, "I'll have eggs for breakfast," or "Where's my shirt?" He's run out of real things to say, and the effort to cover up his emptiness, even with small talk, has become too much for him.

"The silence is deadly," a sixty-two-year-old wife told me. "I can't live with a situation where he just clams up. We grow farther apart every day. It's worse than living alone because I'm so hurt by his silence that when we do talk, I say things I shouldn't say, and he says things he shouldn't say, and it's awful. Is this what I must expect as I grow older?"

It's not.

The silence barrier is what causes many retirement marriages to go wrong. But you can break that barrier.

How can you break the silence barrier?

You must first become emotionally mature for retirement. Then you must put your emotional maturity to work for you. You can do that in three steps.

BY KNOWING YOURSELF BETTER

As an emotionally mature retiree, you know yourself. That is, you know the positive and the negative emotions that dominate your retirement life; you found that out by following the guidelines in chapter 3. Now get to know yourself better.

Ask yourself, What is it about my spouse that arouses my positive emotions? my negative ones? Or, putting it another way, What traits in my spouse give me emotional satisfaction? emotional dissatisfaction? Keep those traits in mind.

BY UNDERSTANDING YOUR SPOUSE'S ROLE IN SOLVING THIS (OR ANY) PROBLEM

You need your spouse to continue exhibiting the traits that give you emotional satisfaction. And you need your spouse to discontinue the traits that give you emotional dissatisfaction. These needs are your emotional needs in marriage.

You couldn't have discovered these needs before if you didn't know yourself before. Now that you know what your emotional needs in marriage are, you have something to talk about.

BY TALKING ABOUT YOUR PROBLEM

At this point, communication with your spouse is necessary.

What happens when you talk about your emotional needs and your spouse is still emotionally immature for retirement?

It would be a pretty one-sided conversation. You'd be carrying on much like a certain actress who was renowned for her ego. She would talk incessantly about herself, then break off sharply and say, "Enough about me. Let's talk about you. What do you think about me?"

A monologue about oneself doesn't break the silence barrier. It could strengthen it. "All he wants to talk about is himself. So what's there for me to say?"

What you have to do is lead your spouse along the path to emotional maturity for retirement. In every marriage situation, one or the other has to be the aggressor. In this situation, it's your turn.

What if you're not the aggressive type? You like yourself and want good things for yourself, don't you? And isn't a happy marriage one of the best things you could possibly want? So get aggressive. Tell your spouse, "Look, if I can achieve emotional maturity, so can you. Remember, there's a lot at stake—the rest of our lives."

What happens when you talk about your emotional needs and your spouse is emotionally mature for retirement?

Your spouse will get to know his or her emotional needs, too, and will talk about them. Now you'll have an important dialogue going on. You'll be talking about your individual selves in relationship with each other. That's because each of you wants to know if your new emotional needs can be satisfied by the other. Did I say that that's an important dialogue? It's the most important dialogue of your married life in retirement.

How do you pinpoint your emotional needs in retirement marriage?

Ask yourself, What qualities does the real "me" need my spouse to exhibit? What qualities doesn't the real me need my spouse to show? That's the same as asking yourself what kind of person you want your spouse to be from now on and what kind of person you don't want him or her to be.

Remember, it's the real me you're talking about, the me who might have been buried under a bushel of responsibilities all your previous married life, the me who's surfaced again—four decades or so wiser. It's a me ready to make tough demands on your spouse. Make them! Your happiness is at stake. So when you set up emotional standards for your spouse, don't pull your punches.

If you have a little trouble setting up those standards (almost all retirees do), this checklist will help you get started.

WHAT ARE YOUR EMOTIONAL NEEDS IN RETIREMENT MARRIAGE?

To give me emotional satisfaction, from now on my spouse should be

1. forgiving (especially when I make blunders)
2. gentle
3. tolerant (especially of my friends and relatives)
4. kind
5. loving (not just in bed but all the time)
6. enthusiastic
7. able to show me he or she likes (as well as loves) me
8. optimistic
9. approving (even of the silly things I do)
10. encouraging

To give me emotional satisfaction, from now on my spouse should not be

1. a penny pincher
2. unable to make up his or her mind
3. a spoilsport
4. prone to anger (sometimes for no apparent reason)
5. unsympathetic
6. a "gloomy Gus"
7. disloyal
8. a nag
9. unable to plan more than a day ahead
10. a clinging vine (especially if he or she saps my emotional energy)

The traits you've checked off are only the tip of the iceberg. Give it some thought and you're likely to come up with seven times as many. Have your spouse complete his or her list as well. Now you both have pinpointed your emotional needs in retirement marriage.

Your list may look like a catalog of emotional needs in marriage at any age. It is. But a big difference may apply to you. At your age, you are likely to be more fully aware of your needs and therefore better able to effectively do something about them.

Can your spouse satisfy all your emotional needs?

No spouse can—ever.

What can you do when your spouse cannot satisfy all your emotional needs?

Let's say your spouse knows himself or herself and has revealed that true self to you. So you know the beauty spots and the warts. But some emotional warts, unlike physical ones, cannot be removed. The particular traits that dissatisfy you cannot be changed.

Don't try to change them. It's a guaranteed way to dynamite your marriage. You're bound to fail, and you'll blame it on your spouse. He or she will feel inadequate and will in turn put the blame for those feelings on your shoulders. The result for both of you is guilt, frustration, anger, and feelings of worthlessness. It's an explosive package of negative emotions so strong that it can blow apart even an emotionally mature marriage.

Do remember your emotionally mature retirement attitude toward marriage: Your spouse has as much right to his or her individuality, flaws and all, as you do to yours. Does that mean you have to put up with those traits that dissatisfy you? Not at all. You need to make a judgment.

Ask yourself, In spite of his (her) character defects, does he (she) supply enough of my emotional needs to make me happy?

If the answer is no, you should strongly consider separation or divorce, if practical.

But if the answer is yes (remember, you can't change him or her, and you have no right to even try), adjust to those traits that dissatisfy you.

How do you know when your spouse satisfies enough of your emotional needs?

You can measure "enough" by taking this brief quiz.

FIND OUT IF YOU'RE WILLING TO ADJUST TO YOUR SPOUSE'S EMOTIONAL DEFICIENCIES
---

1. Do you bring your husband or wife gifts from time to time, especially little things he or she likes?

2. Does it give you a glow to show your spouse off to new friends and acquaintances?

3. Are you lonely when he or she goes off on a trip by himself or herself?

4. Do you dream up things to do and places to go to make life more interesting for him or her?

5. Do you really like your spouse—emotional warts and all?

6. Does the thought of life without him or her frighten you?

7. Do you like to touch him or her?

8. Does he or she make you feel like setting new goals in life for both of you?

9. Do you have complete confidence and trust in your husband or wife?

10. Do you make it a point at least once a day to tell your spouse how wonderful he or she is?

If you answered seven or more of these questions yes, you're in love with your spouse! (Yes, at your age. Yes, after all these years.) And that means there's no question but that he or she satisfies enough of your emotional needs. You're more than willing to adjust to his or her emotional deficiencies. Just let somebody try to stop you! Love is the basis of a successful marriage.

Are you lifting your eyebrows at the idea of being in love at your age? It's different from before, but it's love. There's less passion, and that means more respect for the other as a human being. That could be the kind of love you've always been looking for. (But that's only one aspect of love as you get older. In chapter 11, you'll learn just how special love can be in later years.)

Is there any other way I can find out if my spouse gives me enough emotional satisfaction?

Yes. It takes a bit of money, and you may have to go through an emotional donnybrook with your spouse before he or she agrees to it, but it could be worth it.

Get away by yourself. Without your husband or wife. Not with relatives, not with friends. Go somewhere where nobody knows you, somewhere you've never been before, somewhere that you know in advance you're going to love. Nothing to remind you of back home. Nothing to dampen your spirits.

Stay until one of two things happen: One, you find (astonishing, but it's true) you don't miss your spouse at all. Or, two, you have to rush home because life is much better with him or her. "Adjust? Just tell me how."

Just how do you adjust to your spouse's emotional deficiencies?

Emotional traits don't exist in a vacuum. They're practical tools for living. The tools work when they solve your marital problems. They don't work when they don't solve them. It's the solutions to these problems that give you emotional satisfaction; the failure to solve them produces emotional dissatisfaction. When your spouse's traits hinder the solution of your marital problems, they're defective tools. Those traits are your spouse's emotional deficiencies.

For example, your husband is unable to make up his mind when it comes to spending or investing money. He's great at collecting facts, organizing them, and even working out three or four possible decisions. But when it comes to making that final decision, he just can't get himself to do it. He has an emotional tool that works part of the way and then breaks down. But you have an emotional need for a spouse who's decisive, who can solve the family's money problems. What should you do?

Here's how you adjust.

Adjustment is a problem like any other. As an emotionally mature retiree, you go through the decision-making process (chapter 5) and come up with an answer. You tell your husband, "From now on, whenever we have a money problem, you gather the facts, you analyze them, and you come up with a number of possible solutions. I'll make the final emotional decision."

You have arranged it so that the two of you together pooled your emotional traits to produce the perfect tool for solving your marital problem. You have achieved emotional satisfaction.

When a marital problem is solved, you get 10 points in emotional satisfaction. It is possible that because of an emotional deficiency, your spouse may supply only 6 in a particular situation. To get the 10 points you need, you've got to supply the other 4. You have to make up yourself for what your spouse lacks emotionally.

When you adjust to your spouse's emotional deficiencies, will your spouse adjust to yours?

If you're two emotionally mature people, yes. But one of you has to start the ball rolling. Don't wait for the other to make the first move (that's false pride). Go after what you want—a happy marriage.

Adjustment requires patience, tact, brainpower, stick-to-it-iveness, self-discipline, and a vast outpouring of emotional energy.

Emotional adjustment seems like real hard work. Is it worth the effort?

Judge for yourself.

- Your adjustments preserve your marriage—and

a life together with someone you love is the greatest of human joys.

· Almost all retirement problems ultimately involve you and your spouse, as you saw in chapters 4 and 5. When you adjust emotionally, you can act as a unit and come up with a single decision that's emotionally satisfactory to both of you. What's more, any decision either of you makes on your own will be emotionally satisfactory to the other; your decision takes into account the adjustments you have to make.

· Emotional adjustment means happiness and companionship in marriage. That, according to Dr. Lynch and many medical authorities, is the prescription for a healthy life and a longer one.

· In retirement, a one-part family unit may replace the three-part family unit of your earlier years (grandchildren, children, and grandparents). The one-part family unit is composed of you and your spouse. You're on your own. You may get help from your scattered family, but don't bank on it. So it's important that you strengthen your family unit's will to survive and prosper. Emotional adjustment provides that strength. You're ready to face the harsh realities of modern existence—harsher for you because you're in retirement—without fear and with hope.

· Your marriage is the center of your retirement universe. When emotional adjustment makes your marriage good, it makes all life good.

Convinced?

Well, if you're not, consider this: It's either adjusting to the person you love and who loves you or smashing that love. It's living in happiness or living in loneliness.

Your move.

Your spouse doesn't give you enough emotional satisfaction. You don't want the inconvenience of physical separation. Can you practice emotional separation instead?

One retiree tells how. "I decided I would live my own life and not even give her a thought. I map out my days as if she weren't in it. All we do is share the same roof. She has her own room; I have my own life. As far as she's concerned, I live my life with blinders on."

Living with blinders on is not uncommon. But I don't know of any retiree who can do it without a sense of cheating and disloyalty, a certain amount of anger bordering on hate, and an intense guilt feeling. These destructive emotions play havoc with your health and peace of mind.

And what about the spouse who's shut out? "You can't imagine how hurt I am. I try to make his life as miserable as he tries to make mine," one wife of a retiree confessed.

Emotional separation as a substitute for physical separation never works; it only makes matters worse. If your spouse can't satisfy enough of your emotional needs, face up to it and part amicably. That's the emotionally mature thing to do in retirement or at any other time of your life.

Your spouse doesn't supply enough of your emotional needs. But you can't physically separate. (There isn't enough money, your religion forbids it, or one of you is ill and needs the other's care.) Is there any way to make your marriage livable?

Yes. Adopt a new emotionally mature retirement attitude: I'll try to control situations to suppress his or her bad traits and bring out the good ones.

If, for example, your wife is kind except when it comes to money, watch your pennies. Her penny-pinching won't get a chance to show, but she'll show her gratitude by being even kinder in other things. (Like being more tolerant of your friends.)

What you're doing is not adjustment. Adjustment means sharing the emotional load associated with solving a marital problem. In this case, she's supplying a gigantic zero. To get the emotional satisfaction you need, you have to come up with the full 10 points yourself. That's not sharing. She's giving nothing. You're giving in.

That means self-denial and the emotional dissatisfaction that comes with it. How, then, do you gain?

In every situation you control, you swap one of her bad traits (like penny-pinching) for one of her good traits (like kindness). The emotional satisfaction you get from the good trait cancels out the emotional dissatisfaction you get from self-denial. Your overall happiness shows no loss, no gain.

But if the good trait you're bringing out in her glows a bit brighter (say, she's kinder), the balance of emotional satisfaction can swing in your favor. Simply stated, you may find yourself somewhat happier for your sacrifice.

It's a limited form of happiness. And since it's based on self-denial, it requires a bulldog determination. You don't get much, and you have to struggle to get it, but it's all the happiness you're going to get when you're trapped in a marriage that doesn't give you the emotional satisfaction you need. The happiness you do get, though, makes that marriage livable—and that could be a springboard to a happier retirement life.

Whether you're emotionally adjusted or not, are there any additional guidelines that can make your retirement marriage happier?

Yes, there are. And they follow.

GUIDELINES FOR A SUCCESSFUL MARRIAGE IN RETIREMENT

---

1. *Don't* let your channels of communication dry up. Understanding each other, which is what communication is all about, is a never-ending job. You and your spouse continue to grow and change. Stop communicating and you become strangers. *Do* remember that you like yourself, so whenever the impulse comes over you to clam up, do something good for yourself. Speak up instead about things that mean something to both of you.

2. *Don't* take your spouse's good traits for granted. *Do* show your appreciation. You know what vitamins can do to perk you up. A compliment is a vitamin in words.

3. *Don't* be brutally frank about your spouse's bad traits. When you're brutally frank, too often you're just brutal. *Do* be understanding, considerate, and, above all, tactful. Remember, you have bad traits of your own, and how would you like it if you had your nose rubbed in them?

4. *Don't* retrench emotionally. If you do, you're conforming to the ageist myth that older married people are emotionally dried-up and joyless. Retirement marriage is no time for emotional belt-tightening. *Do* live your emotional life to the fullest. Have

fun, get excited, get involved, and get high on just doing things you want to do and were never able to do before. And, most of all, laugh. If you'll just let yourself go, you'll be amazed at what a kick out of life two emotionally adjusted retired people can get together.

5. *Don't* ask your children's advice on your marriage problems; even the best-adjusted marriage has them. *Do* solve your problems yourself. There's nobody better equipped than you to do it.

6. *Don't* make emotional allies of your children. There are bad days in any marriage, and that's when you're likely to run off to one or another of your children for sympathy. All that will do is rupture the closeness in the family. Your children will still be taking sides long after you and your spouse have made up. *Do* turn your bad days into good days by talking things out with each other.

7. *Don't* go to the aid of your children in an emergency unless you consult with your spouse. If you don't bring your spouse into the picture, he or she may feel suspicious, left out, and resentful. Chances are that you'd make a decision your spouse would approve of, but why risk brewing that kettle of negative emotions? *Do* make all your decisions concerning help to your children jointly.

8. *Don't* belittle or ridicule your spouse's ideas (no matter how silly they seem). That's an invitation to your spouse to climb back behind the silence barrier. *Do* be a good listener. A person can talk and say nothing; so can a person listen and hear nothing. You don't hear ideas with your ears; you hear them with your mind. Keep it open. There's some merit in any idea. Find it and tell your spouse about it. That will

keep him or her talking, and sooner or later your spouse will come up with an idea you'll be proud of.

9. *Don't* regard married life as a grim undertaking, with every little mishap to be analyzed and pondered. *Do* cultivate a sense of humor. Learn to laugh at yourself and with each other when the daily snags of living together threaten to get you down.

10. *Don't* squelch your spouse's dreams. Retirement can be the time to make them come true. Now your spouse has the time, the freedom, the right attitudes, and the emotional energy to realize them. *Do* get inside your spouse's dreams so that you can share his or her enthusiasm. Then help your spouse to make his or her dreams feasible. Remember, you have dreams of your own, and you could use some help, too, to make them come true.

11. *Don't* succumb to the myth that sex dies in retirement. Believe that myth and you'll be buying a self-fulfilling prophecy. You'll mentally turn off to sex forever, though you're still able emotionally and physically to carry on. *Do* realize that sex can go on, and it can be vital to you that it does. Love is the basis of a successful marriage, and sex is an important way to show your love. Sex in later years can be wonderful—so wonderful that a whole chapter (chapter 11) is devoted to it.

12. *Don't* get into a marriage rut. When two people are with each other twenty-four hours a day, he's likely to forget to shave and she's likely to come to breakfast with rollers in her hair. Those may be symptoms of letting go. *Do* regard marriage in retirement as a second courtship. Dress up. Be up. Stay up again (well, at least once) to see the sunrise, locked in each other's arms. You get the point. Life

can be beautiful whenever you start to live. Start now!

Your emotionally mature retirement attitude to marriage is: Each spouse has the right to do his or her own thing. Isn't that disruptive?

Just the reverse.

Remember, you move into emotional maturity by knowing yourself and then by being yourself. So does your spouse. Being yourself is part of doing your own thing. When two people are themselves, not performing or putting on an act, in the company of each other, they are having one of the warmest experiences of life. Dr. William Gass describes it: "To freely give and freely to receive, to live an open life with at least one another in an atmosphere of acceptance and trust—secretless . . . what an extraordinary achievement . . . what exhilaration to have one's spirit finally freed . . . what a priceless gift."

You were never closer.

It's this closeness that gives you the freedom to be away from each other and to pursue your own interests without disrupting your marriage.

You can express this freedom in small things. "I like going to a restaurant with a friend," one retiree told me. "I like to shop alone. I like to walk alone, sometimes. I like to eat alone—rarely, but when I have to get to myself to think things out. I like to go to X-rated movies alone."

Or you can express it in big things. You can pursue a new career, go back to school, travel, attain spiritual enlightenment, work at realizing your full potential as a human being, or reach for new goals.

You have a life of your own within the boundaries of your marriage. With the approval and the encouragement of your spouse, you live alone—together.

It is a preparation for that solemn moment when you must live alone—all alone. That's the moment when death comes, as it must, to your spouse.

It's a moment that you've thrust back into the deep recesses of your mind. Like almost all retirees, you refuse to face the thought of your spouse's death. Or your own. In the next chapter, I'll show you how to face up to your fear of death and deal with it—and open the door to even greater happiness in retirement.

9

How to Deal with Your Fear of Death

A researcher for this book interviewed retirement counselors for the nation's largest corporations. He asked them, "Why don't you add a session on preparation for death to your retirement-planning program?"

The answer he invariably received was "Nobody would come. And it would sour them on the rest of the program."

Retirees don't want to think about death. And that probably includes you.

What's so bad about not wanting to think about death? It's not a pleasant topic, is it?

It's not. But hiding the thought of your death and the death of your spouse can make your life miserable, no matter what else you do to make it happy.

Why will hiding the thought of death make your life miserable?

There are two reasons.

ANXIETY

"Repression of death," writes psychoanalyst Dr. Norman O. Brown, "results in anxiety." Dr. Brown uses *anxiety* in its pathological sense. In that sense, anxiety is to worry what cancer is to a wart. It is one of the worst emotional diseases because its psychosomatic effects can be ruinous. But anxiety poses an even greater danger—it can deprive you of the will to live. By repressing the thought of death, you could hasten your real death.

GUILT

You abhor coming face to face with a dying person because you'd like the thought of death to stay hidden. So you go along with the way our society treats the dying. They're often shut away to die in remote isolation wards of hospitals. The glittering array of science's medical instrumentation doesn't replace the touch of a loving hand. Yet you transfer your responsibility to comfort your dying friends and relatives to the frequently cold care of health professionals.

As a result, you feel an overwhelming sense of guilt that can be almost as destructive to your health as anxiety. It can crop up in many different neurotic forms.

Anxiety and guilt are negative emotions. Why can't you put them to work for you as you would any other negative emotion?

You put your negative emotions to work for you to start you on the decision-making process that solves your problem. But in order to do that, you must know what your problem is. In this case, you don't. You've hidden your problem. Psychoanalysts would say you've buried the thought of death in your subconscious. You can put the negative emotions you feel in this case to work for you only when you've brought the thought of death out into the open. You must consciously accept it.

How can I consciously accept the thought of my death and the death of my spouse?

Apply your emotionally mature attitude toward health: Serious illness can strike at any time. The word *serious* could mean mortal. It could mean incurable. Your attitude implies death can strike at any time. You consciously accept the thought of death when you're emotionally mature.

Even if you're emotionally mature, it's often difficult to accept the thought of death. Is there some way that can help?

Yes, and it can be an important way. It's well illustrated by two stories told by Dr. Paul Niehans, an eminent European authority on biological aging.

Niehans and his father, the chief surgeon of Berne, Switzerland, observed an operation during which a patient died after receiving an overdose of anesthetic. The white sheet had already been placed over the body when Niehans's father made an effort to revive the dead man with heart massage. He succeeded. The man had been medically dead—no heartbeat, no respiration, and no brain waves—for an hour.

The younger Niehans describes the experience. " 'How was it' I asked him. 'There was no pain,' he said.

'I felt as if I were going through a tunnel at the end of which I saw a clear light. I wasn't anxious at all. On the contrary. Suddenly I felt somebody grab me by the neck and pull me backwards away from the light. Then I woke up.' "

Several years later, Paul Niehans revived a man who had drowned in Lake Geneva, Switzerland. The man had been medically dead for thirty minutes. He told Niehans exactly what the other revived man had told him. He described the complete absence of pain, the tunnel, the light—everything.

"Since then," Niehans says, "I haven't given death a second thought."

Dr. Elisabeth Kübler-Ross, an internationally respected researcher in the field of life after death, claims that she, too, has proof of life after death on the basis of hundreds of such stories. Some medical authorities hold that her witnesses, suffering the shock of near death, merely hallucinated their alleged after-death experiences. "If you have a woman who has been declared dead in a hospital, and she can tell you exactly how many people walked into the room and worked on her, this cannot be hallucination," Dr. Kübler-Ross argues.

Her interviewees corroborated the stories told by Niehans's patients with respect to the absence of pain, the tunnel, and the light. It seems as if all "dead" people who have been revived share a common afterlife experience. This finding has been confirmed by Dr. Raymond A. Moody, Jr., through his in-depth interviews with fifty persons pronounced medically dead as a result of accident, illness, or sudden cardiac arrest.

What are your emotional experiences likely to be after death? Dr. Kübler-Ross sums up the common feelings: a deep sense of calm and well-being and a feeling of wholeness (people who have lost limbs or other parts of their bodies, as in a mastectomy, feel whole again).

"Many . . . resented our desperate attempts to bring them back to life," she reports. "Death is the feeling of peace and hope. Not one of them has ever been afraid to die again."

If you can believe in life after death in order to help you accept the thought of death, do so. These pioneering discoveries by scientists, though not generally accepted by the scientific community, may give support to your belief. If you are very religious, you may not need scientific support. Many retirees who've lost touch with the religion of their childhood return to it in old age. It gives them the faith in the afterlife that they need to help them accept the thought of death.

You can't believe in life after death. Is there any other way to help you accept the thought of death?

Yes, there is. A swelling body of scientific evidence points to this remarkable fact: Nature prepares you for death by giving you a sense of euphoria, a heightened feeling of well-being, when death is about to come.

"It is . . . probable that the approach of natural death," writes the great Elie Metchnikoff, Russian authority on biological aging, "is accompanied by one of the softest sensations known."

One woman, just hours before her death, wrote: "I feel a great wave of emotion sweep over me. It isn't joy or sorrow. It's a sense of calm—no, more than calm—a feeling that all is right."

Metchnikoff tells of a ninety-three-year-old woman who thirty minutes before her death said, "If you ever reach my age, you will see that death becomes a need, just like sleep."

"Many people," reports psychologist William Sheldon, "often enjoy anticipation of death.... They are frequently observed by the attending intern to die smilingly, as if about to keep a pleasantly anticipated appointment." In the days when they kept a vigil at the side of deathbeds, physicians reported rapturous, transfixed expressions on the faces of the dying.

Nature, it would appear, readies you for the ultimate stage of your life by making it easy for you. It makes the final passage free of mental pain and anguish. It empties you of despair. It fills you with buoyant hope. If you let nature take its course, death ceases to be an enigma wrapped in dread. It becomes a normal, and possibly a surprisingly pleasant, last phase of life.

"One ... who regards death ... not as a supreme misfortune to be painfully endured," writes Robert S. de Ropp, an authority on aging, "will derive from his existence the greatest benefit. As long as his life continues, he will enjoy its pleasures. When death comes, he will greet it with a smile."

It's an unusual idea that nature actually provides you with a peak experience, a feeling of euphoria, in the hours or days before you die. But it does have some scientific backing. When you can believe in it, your anticipation of the pain and the terror accompanying dying will lessen. That should help you accept the thought of death.

Although the attitude in many hospitals toward the dying is changing, don't expect doctors to help you come to an acceptance of the thought of death. Tabitha M. Powledge, a research associate at the Institute of Society, Ethics, and the Life Sciences, writes: "Dying patients [are] ignored as much as possible.... One study has shown that physicians are not only more afraid of death than other people are but also that they fear death even more than people who are terminally ill."

How does accepting the thought of death benefit you?

This acceptance provides you with three things.

RECOGNITION THAT YOU HAVE A PROBLEM

Awareness of death makes you ask, "How can I live my life best when I know I'm going to die?" Now you can put your emotions of anxiety to work for you to start you on the solution to that problem. When you do that, those violently destructive negative emotions can no longer work against you. Your body and your mind are freed from their crippling attacks. They can't stifle your will to live. The removal of stress can add years to your life. Healthy, alert, and determined to live as long as you can, you're now able to start to come to a decision that will solve your problem.

ABILITY TO COME TO A DECISION

You are aware that death is inevitable and that you're in your retirement years. That's an emotionally mature retirement attitude, and on the basis of that attitude, you reach this decision:

Do it now!

If you want to make a dream come true, do it now. If you want to reach for happiness, do it now. If you want to strive for self-fulfillment, do it now. All the things you've always wanted to do and never got around to doing —do them now.

The acceptance of the thought of death can fill your life with pleasurable activities that you might otherwise have put off. But don't fall into the trap of "Eat, drink, and be merry, for tomorrow we die." As an emotionally mature retiree, you are keenly aware of the necessity of keeping your mental, physical, and emotional health at peak levels. You may live to ninety or more! There's time enough to spare to make a rewarding life for yourself instead of throwing it away on dissipation.

Few retirees fall into that trap, but retirement counselors tell me that one out of six retirees fall into another trap. It's the "What's the use, I'll be dead soon anyway" one. They just give up.

Is that what you want to do? Or do you want to accept death as part of life and be part of a world filled with excitement and promise—a world that's alive?

REALIZATION OF THE VALUE OF TIME

This is actually a spin-off on your decision to do it now. Possibly for the first time in your life, you realize how valuable time is. You refuse to throw it away. You won't let trivia rob you of precious hours. "[The acceptance of] death," asserts Barbara Meyerhoff, an anthropologist at the University of California, "can be a great consciousness raiser." You put higher values on everything you do. You won't settle for anything but the best from yourself, and you encourage the best in other people.

Does being aware of the benefits derived from accepting the thought of death have anything to do with conquering your fear of death?

Everything.

Now you understand that death has two meanings. It's an act of nature about which you can do nothing. But it's also a thought, an emotional concept, over which you have complete control. When you repress the thought of death, you can ruin your life—and possibly shorten it. When you accept the thought of death, you can enrich your life—and perhaps prolong it.

Since you like yourself and want the best for yourself, you must accept the thought of death. That starts an emotional chain reaction. To accept the thought of death, you must stop repressing it. What causes that repression? Your fear of death. So to stop repressing your thought of death, you must get rid of the fear of death. To do it, your positive emotions go to work for you and create a new emotionally mature retirement attitude: The act of death is a natural part of life. When it comes, I will accept it because I know nature will prepare me for it. Death holds no terrors. There is nothing to fear.

Does your acceptance of the thought of death change your attitude to the dying?

Yes. This woman's story dramatizes that change.

"I admit now that I was frightened of death. A dear friend of mine was dying in a hospital. I visited her reluctantly. I think she could see how I felt. She said to me—I'll never forget her words—'There's no sunshine outside, and there's no sunshine inside of me. My friends have deserted me.'

"I didn't know what to say. I just wanted to get out of there. I said good-bye quickly and left.

"Now that I accept the thought of death, I'm not afraid of death, afraid of seeing it. I never could turn my back on the dying again. I feel older people who have conquered their fear of death have a responsibility to help others who have not."

Your new emotionally mature attitude to the dying is: I want to comfort them and ease their fear. There are some things to remember when in the presence of a dying person.

GUIDELINES FOR VISITING THE DYING
---

1. *Don't* be falsely cheerful. The dying person can feel the insincerity and won't be comforted. He or she will think less of you.

2. *Don't* waste time in small talk. Time is all the dying person has left. He or she wants to listen to things that are personally meaningful. If you know what they are, don't hesitate to talk about them.

3. *Don't* bring useless presents just for the sake of bringing presents. It will seem as if you are bringing them out of a sense of duty, not love. Be thoughtful. If he or she adores roses, one rose may be the finest gift in the world.

4. *Don't* avoid the subject of death or use euphemisms such as "passing on" or "when you leave us." It's hard not to do because evading the words *death* and *dying* is a deep-rooted custom in our society, and talking about death is an unwritten taboo. You want to help your friend or relative lose the fear of death, and speaking honestly about death is the way to do it.

5. *Don't* say, "You had a full life. You have much to be thankful for." That's an empty cliché. At the very moment you're saying it, he or she may be wishing, "Oh, what a wasted life! If only I had it to live over again!" Your comment will sadden him or her.

6. *Do* clasp hands, touch, and kiss. There's

nothing more precious than a demonstration of love if you truly feel it.

7. *Do* tell the person how at peace you feel since you accepted the idea of death. Emphasize how easy nature is likely to make it for him or her in the last hours.

8. *Do* show your grief. Cry if you must. It's another sign of love. A stony face may signal "I don't care." It's fashionable to control yourself, but self-control in this case can be a cruel insult to the dying person. On the other hand, don't lose control, either. You don't want to agitate the person.

9. *Do* speak in your usual voice. Hushed tones are for funerals, not for the living.

10. *Do* stay as long as you can even though neither speaks. From Freud on, psychologists have known that your very presence speaks. If you are loving, the dying person will feel your love. If you have conquered your fear of death, the dying person will absorb some of your serenity. Love and peace of mind are the greatest comforts you can give the dying.

You may be able to accept the thought of your own death and the death of your spouse. But you still fear what the death of your spouse can bring you—loneliness.

As an emotionally mature retiree, you have nothing to fear. In the next chapter, I'll show you how to grow from loneliness to happiness.

10

How to Turn Loneliness into Happiness

"My husband died . . . and for two years I was just as crazy as you can be," reveals Helen Hayes, one of the nation's most honored actresses. "I didn't have any really normal minutes during those two years. It wasn't just grief. It was total confusion."

Here was a woman who had built a stunningly successful career for herself in one of the most competitive industries in the world, show business. She was fifty-seven when her husband died, and up to that time, she had been, in her own words, "infallible . . . arrogant. . . . Why did God give me the gift of being so right so much of the time?"

Yet in those first two husbandless years, this self-assured woman was incapable of making up her mind about anything. She became nervous, frightened, and timid. The day-in, day-out decisions necessary for survival in the theater were too much for her.

She was the victim of loneliness.

But it's not only the widowed who are vulnerable.

Anybody can be lonely. And retirees can be especially lonely.

How lonely are you?

Find out for yourself by answering the following questions yes or no. At the end of the questionnaire, you'll learn how to evaluate your loneliness score and what your score means.

YOUR LONELINESS SCORE
---

1. Do you feel your spouse no longer satisfies many of your emotional needs?

2. Do you miss your job (and that includes the job of bringing up a family)?

3. Do you sometimes feel that you are all by yourself when you're among friends and neighbors?

4. Do you long to give somebody a real warm hug and kiss and get one in return?

5. Do you feel like a stranger in the presence of younger people?

6. Do you wish there was at least one person who could make you feel good?

7. Do you sometimes feel out of it in group activities (community gatherings, political meetings, and so on)?

8. Do you believe the world has passed you by?

9. Do you feel you'll never find anyone who understands your views?

10. When you're with people, are you confused, filled with self-doubts, depressed, frightened, or outraged?

11. Do you ever feel a sharp ache in the chest when you're alone?

12. Are you being worn down by a dull feeling that you can't seem to shake?

Here's how to find your loneliness score.

For every yes, give yourself 5 points. Give yourself an additional 30 points for a yes to question 10, 50 points for a yes to question 11, and 60 points for a yes to question 12.

Here's what your loneliness score means.

A score of 60 or less means you're lonely but not dangerously so. The lower your score, the less lonely you are. If you scored 0, you're one of the most fortunate of human beings—you're not lonely.

A score of 65 to 90 means you're approaching the danger zone.

A score of 95 to 200 means you're dangerously lonely. Your mental and physical health could break down.

If you scored more than 0, don't think you're unusual. "Loneliness," observes Dr. Robert S. Weiss, a psychiatrist at Harvard University, "appears to be almost as prevalent as colds during winter." Many retirees suffer from loneliness.

Low to moderate degrees of loneliness (loneliness scores up to 90) will not seriously affect your ability to function as a normal human being. But once the danger zone is reached (loneliness scores higher than 110), loneliness can drain your emotional energy, sap your will to live, and batter your body with disruptive stresses. Dangerous loneliness, warns Rex

Taylor, expert on aging, "must now be regarded as a killer in the same category as diseases receiving wide media attention."

But don't feel too smug if your loneliness score is low (scores of 5 to 60). In a recent survey, a majority of retirees agreed that loneliness increases as you age. Dangerous loneliness could lurk in your future if you don't do something about it now.

How widespread is dangerous loneliness?

In one survey of retirees living in California, 16 percent admitted they were "very lonely" (dangerously so). In another survey, one out of five retirees reported they suffered loneliness to "a heartbreaking degree." While major degenerative diseases, including senility and heart disease, strike only about 5 percent of the nation's retirees, dangerous loneliness incapacitates 20 percent or more.

What are the symptoms of dangerous loneliness?

In dangerous loneliness, you become painfully aware of yourself as incomplete because you're without an emotional link to another human being. You're moved by an excruciating longing to feel somebody, anybody, close to you—to touch, to talk, to share emotions. A driving passion for human warmth chases everything else from your mind.

Your ambitions, hopes, vitality, desires, and dreams may vanish. Stripped of them, your life seems without value. Doubts about your self-worth assail you. You're confused, terrified, and saddled with anxiety.

There seems no way out of your trap. "It's like being in solitary confinement," one sixty-eight-year-old man lamented. "Nobody helps." You feel boxed in, abandoned, and deprived. Your frustration explodes in bursts of anger. You become hostile and cantankerous. But your rage only drives people farther away. Hopelessness envelops you. You sink into despair. You feel that life isn't worth living.

Your emotional distress can devastate your body. Sharp pains knife through your chest. Your legs feel weak and hollow. Often you hurt deep in your stomach. Your senses are numbed. It seems that the nerves to and from your brain have been frozen. You feel worn out and fatigued.

Dangerous loneliness can leave an imprint of misery on your features, your speech, and your manner. Your shoulders become stooped. Your mouth turns down at the corners. Your eyes cloud with sadness. Your voice grows feeble and hoarse. Your walk is so slow it appears painful. You become crotchety and withdrawn.

Dangerous loneliness has been known to result in breakdowns, divorce, alcoholism, and even drug addiction and suicide.

What causes dangerous loneliness?

The same emotional problems that cause loneliness. Dangerous loneliness is prolonged and aggravated loneliness.

What emotional problems cause loneliness?

There are two. One is the unsatisfied need for loving emotional responses from another human being. The other is the unsatisfied need to touch, and be touched with love by, another human being.

When you solve these two problems, you solve the problem of loneliness, including dangerous loneliness.

Can you be lonely when you're with people?

Of course. When your two basic antiloneliness needs —the need for loving emotional responses and the need to touch, and be touched, with love—are unsatisfied, you're lonely. You've been with people before who satisfied neither of these needs. When you're with people of that sort, you're lonely.

You can be lonely with friends when they do no more than share your entertainment with you. You can be a joiner and still be lonely when you want more from club members than participation in their activities. You can even be lonely with your family when they take you for granted and ignore you emotionally. ("I've never felt so lonely," many retired men and women have told me, "as at our family parties.") You can be lonely in a crowd.

It's not being with people that cures your loneliness. It's being with people who satisfy your two basic antiloneliness needs.

What are the loving emotional responses you need?

Let your mind go back over the past few hours. You might have chatted with your husband or wife, the supermarket checkout person, your next-door neighbor, the mail carrier, or a friend. Ask yourself, Didn't I want them to display some emotional response that showed I meant something to them? This could be tenderness, warmth, humor, merriment, or interest. Or shared sorrow or anger. Of course, you did.

Those are loving emotional responses, and there are hundreds of them. What specific response you need at any time depends on the kind of person you are and the situation you find yourself in. You may need admiration to heighten the joy of success. You may need sympathy to soften the blow of failure. Or you may just need a good laugh to make time go faster.

A dependable flow of loving emotional responses is as basic to your well-being as food and drink, shelter, and sex. You live happily and healthily only insofar as you receive the loving emotional satisfaction you need.

How do you ask for a specific emotional response?

You don't do it by speaking up. Just imagine yourself saying to a snooty salesclerk, "I need you to be tender to me." If you're like many retirees, you won't say it even to your husband or wife.

And if you tried to express your emotional needs in words, you might find it difficult to do. You were brought up in a generation that frowned on talking about emotions, and that training may have stuck with you. You regard speaking about your feelings as you do using four-letter words. It's embarrassing and indecent.

That's a pity. In our dehumanized times, emotional satisfaction from other human beings is rarer than ever, which is one reason why loneliness as a social disease may soon reach epidemic proportions. Speaking about your unsatisfied emotional needs without beating about the bush could make it easier for people you know to speak about their own unsatisfied emotional needs. The impersonality of many human relations could thaw into a personal exchange of human feelings.

It's to be desired. But it doesn't always happen. In the meantime, we all fall back on three indirect ways of asking for the loving emotional responses that satisfy our needs.

USING THE SILENT LANGUAGE OF THE BODY

You do it all the time, whether you're aware of it or not. When you have an emotional need, your body sends out a signal. That signal can be a tear ("I need comforting"). Or it can be an expectant smile ("I need approval"). Or it can be a nervous drumming with your fingertips ("I need to be calmed down"). It can be an enormous variety of gestures, postures, expressions, changes of skin tone, and movements. These signals make up the silent language of the body.

That language can be as easy to understand as a comic strip's (you have no trouble getting the message when the driver of the car you've just passed shakes his fist at you). Or it can be as fine-drawn as the smile on the Mona Lisa and just as hard to figure out.

Most body signals are subtle. Dr. Domenick A. Barbara, a psychiatrist specializing in communications, gives this dramatic example: "A courting woman is apt to play with her hair, stroking it or twining a strand about one finger. [She looks at the man], holding her head to one side, her pelvis tipped up and forward. The man is apt to stand with his pelvis rolled back." The bodies of both are speaking seductively of love and sex.

"People," adds Dr. Barbara, "are always demonstrating their innermost feelings toward each other . . . with their bodies." According to Dr. Barbara, psychologists estimate that at least 65 percent of all emotional exchanges are carried on through the silent language of the body.

USING THE HIDDEN LANGUAGE OF IDEAS

From childhood on, you were encouraged to put your ideas into words and to take a stand on the issues affecting your life and the lives of all the people around you. And you do both still, perhaps better now than ever before because you've had so many years to practice. But when you're talking about issues, it's not only ideas you're talking about.

When you tell others that you've thought the whole thing out and such and such should be done, you could be looking for applause, a glow of affection, sexual approval, or many other kinds of satisfaction from a long catalog of loving emotional responses. Your most carefully reasoned arguments can in actuality be hidden ways of transmitting your emotional needs. "Only a fool," asserts British writer Alida Greydanus, "would dispute the notion that out of the heart still spring all the important issues of life." In ordinary conversation, the expression of ideas frequently serves the same purpose as body language—the conveying of emotional needs.

USING THE MUSICAL LANGUAGE OF THE VOICE

How often have you remarked, "It's not what she said; it's how she said it"? The human voice can plead, beguile, entice, or cajole while the words that emerge are as plain as bread and butter. It's with the musical language (the tones, rhythms, pauses, and melodies) of your voice that you make your requests for loving emotional responses. Your words alone too often speak another language that says nothing to the heart.

These three kinds of language make up one language

used by people everywhere at all times—the language of the emotions. It is with this language that you signal your requests for the loving emotional responses you need.

How does receiving the loving emotional responses you need from another human being help end your loneliness?

When you send out a signal of emotional need and there's no response, or when the emotional response you elicit runs counter to your emotional need, there is no emotional linkage with another person. You feel cut off, isolated. It is as if you were alone. You're lonely. But when you receive the emotional response you need, you've made an emotional linkage with another person. You're no longer separate, by yourself. You're no longer lonely.

Why do you need to touch, and be touched lovingly by, another human being?

You're a woman. Close your eyes and think of the most vivid memory of your husband. If you're a man, do the same for your wife. What is it? His physique? His voice? His distinctive scent? His taste when you kiss him? Or isn't it, rather, his hands on you? His caresses? His fingers as they stroke your hair? His *touch*? "What I miss most," a widow told me, "is not feeling his body next to me at night." The most powerful impressions made on you are made by touch. And you make your most powerful impressions the same way.

There's a profound reason for this. No happy human relationship can exist, the celebrated psychoanalyst Bruno Bettelheim has discovered, without loving touch. Psychoanalyst Frieda Fromm-Reichmann says that the longing for touching, and being touched, lovingly "stays with every human being from infancy thoughout life; and there is no human being who is not threatened by its loss." To touch, and to be touched, with love is a human need as fundamental as eating, drinking, and mating. It is as basic as the need for loving emotional responses.

The English language reflects the stunning impact of touch on our emotional lives. When we touch, we say we "feel." Touching becomes an emotional experience, a "feeling." When we are moved, deeply affected, we say we're "touched." We talk about "getting in touch." When you are lonely, you "lose touch" with humanity.

Touching, and being touched, with love is not just a physical linkage with another being; it's an emotional one. The lonely person reaches out for the touch of a human hand, and it isn't there.

Touch is also a form of body language. The handshake is a time-honored way of breaking down the barrier between strangers. When the late President Lyndon B. Johnson was asked why he was such a great hugger, he replied, "I must feel a man's skin to know him."

Through touch, you can send out your message of emotional need with greater intensity than by any other form of emotional language. When you're blocked off from human touch, there's less chance of that message getting through and more chance that your need for loving emotional responses will go unsatisfied. Losing physical touch makes emotional contact with others that much more difficult.

Is loneliness in retirement different from loneliness at any other time of life?

Not basically. The need for loving emotional responses and the need to touch, and be touched, lovingly are present throughout your life. When these two antiloneliness needs are unsatisfied, you're lonely at any age.

Since the causes of loneliness are the same at all stages of life, so is the cure. The emotional attitudes that solve the problem of loneliness are not exclusively emotionally mature retirement attitudes. They're used by people of all ages.

In retirement, however, there are more kinds of loneliness than before, and loneliness can be more painful than at any other time of life.

What are the different kinds of loneliness in retirement?

There are seven potential sources for your two fundamental antiloneliness needs as you enter retirement. If these sources are cut off from you, you experience seven different kinds of loneliness.

1. You're lonely for your children if they move away or if you move away from them.

2. You're lonely for your fellow workers when your working years are over.

3. You're lonely for your friends and neighbors if they slip out of your life.

4. You're lonely for the wife or husband of your middle years if a barrier of silence comes between you.

5. You're lonely for younger people if you feel like an alien in their world.

6. You're lonely for your older relatives when death depletes their ranks.

7. You're lonely for your dead husband or wife.

Why can loneliness in older years be more painful than at any other time of life?

When all the kinds of retirement loneliness that you are vulnerable to strike at the same time, and they can as you grow older, you're overcome by all the symptoms of dangerous loneliness.

"Anyone who has encountered persons who were under the influence of real loneliness," reports Fromm-Reichmann, "understands why older people are more frightened of being lonely than of being without food, or being deprived of sleep, or having their sexual needs unfulfilled." As you grow older, you can come face to face with what has been called "the naked horror of total loneliness."

Psychologist Ira J. Tanner asserts, "It is possible to die of a broken heart, and hearts may break when all former sources of attention and love are gone."

How can you end loneliness?

Take two steps to satisfy your antiloneliness needs. The first step is to get other people to give you the loving emotional responses you need, and the second step is to get yourself to touch others, and get others to touch you, with love.

How can you take the first step to end loneliness—getting people to give you the loving emotional responses you need?

Adopt the first of the new emotionally mature attitudes to deal with loneliness: I must give loving emotional responses to others to get loving emotional responses from them.

When you give others the loving emotional responses they need, a wonderful thing may happen—you may get the emotional responses you need in return.

But before you can give loving emotional responses to others, you must understand just what responses they need in specific situations. To do that, you must learn to read the language of emotions. Because it is composed of a silent language of the body, a hidden language of ideas, and a musical language of the voice, it may appear to be a difficult language to master. It's not. The following guidelines will help.

**GUIDELINES FOR
READING THE LANGUAGE OF EMOTIONS**
---

1. Don't jump to conclusions based on preconceived notions of what the other person is like. You must see other people's emotional needs as they are and not as you think they should be.

2. Give the other person your full attention and interest. Sometimes we read only what we want to read and discard everything else. (Try an experiment. Make a tape of any of your conversations. Before you play it back, make notes of what you think you heard. Now play back the tape. Listen carefully and compare what you think you heard with what you're actually hearing. You may find you have heard as little as one-third of the message.) Unless you make a complete reading, you're likely to miss the essential signals.

3. Forget about your own emotional needs for the moment. You can get so involved with your own needs that you have no patience to learn about anyone else's. Your emotional needs stand like a screen in the way of the other person's signals. When you remove your own emotional needs from your mind, you open your mind to the other's needs.

4. Meet with another person when and where there are no distractions. Noise and bustle make it difficult for you to concentrate. For that reason, some restaurants are poor places to get to know somebody emotionally. Cocktail parties are even worse. A quiet walk together or a tête-à-tête over a cup of coffee or tea works wonders when you're trying to read another person's emotional needs.

5. Respect the other person's emotional needs. Don't nullify what you read in another because you think it's too trivial to consider seriously. An emotional demand for childish fun can be just as important as a longing for a release from grief. Don't impose your standards. Accept the other person's. Remember that every person is an individual in his or her own right, with a personal catalog of desires, wishes, passions, and fantasies—just like you.

6. Be patient. Emotional signals aren't transmitted in a steady stream. Concentrate on the other person, keep your mind open, and wait. When the signals come, you'll be able, after some practice, to recognize them.

7. Encourage the other person to transmit his or her signals freely, by bringing a warm curiosity to your meetings. Wanting to get to know your companion by means of tactful and friendly questions will please the other person. Almost everybody likes to talk about himself or herself. The emotional signals you're looking for should come through.

8. Don't be afraid of silences. If the other person wants to muse for a few moments, don't interrupt with "Well, what else is new?" or other inconsequential remarks just to keep the conversation going. Look instead for the body language—glances, expressions, the play of muscles under the skin—which speaks as well.

9. **Read between the lines.** Don't get hung up on what's being said. It's how it's being said that counts. And, remember, if ideas are being discussed, look for the emotional response the person is trying to evoke with those ideas.

And, most important,

10. **Don't worry about having to learn a whole new language.** You pick up the language of emotions intuitively. Keep your mind open.

You'll have less trouble reading the language of emotions when you understand the attitudes behind it. (The discussion in chapter 7 on attitudes in relation to dealing with younger people can be applied to others as well.) An emotionally mature couple seem to be able to read each other's minds. But when you don't have a grasp of other people's attitudes, rely on intuition to decode their emotional needs. It's slower, and you'll make mistakes at first, but after a while you'll get the knack.

When you know what loving emotional responses another person needs, give them. Give them freely, with warmth and affection. That's what giving of yourself is all about.

How can you take the second step to end loneliness—getting yourself to touch people, and getting people to touch you, with love?

You have a new antiloneliness attitude: I must give loving emotional responses to others to get loving emotional responses from them. Put it to work for you. When you do, you make a friend. A real friend. The interchange of loving emotional responses is the real meaning of friendship.

When you link yourself to another human being in the emotional tie of real friendship, loving touches are exchanged naturally. A hand on a hand. A kiss of greeting. Arms around each other's shoulders. Walking arm in arm. Reaching for each other as you talk. The pressure and warmth of touch is one of the special joys of real friendship.

Don't fight it. Many retirees do. They might have been brought up to regard touching any human being other than a member of the family as bad-mannered, if not obscene. All their lives, touching others might have been surrounded by taboos and restrictions. If your natural desire to touch, and be touched, lovingly has been frozen by your early training, it's time to thaw it out.

Make an effort not to shrink back when your friend attempts to touch you. It will help if you remember that your friend's touch is a way of saying "How glad I am that we're friends!" Try to let yourself go, instead. And when you feel the desire to hold out your hand to your friend, do so. You'll be giving pleasure to your friend as well as to yourself. There's nothing like a heartwarming embrace to bring two people together emotionally. If you're shy, remember that, according to Dr. Barbara, the natural way older people express their affection is with a hug.

Now you know how to satisfy your two antiloneliness needs when you're with other people. But what happens when you're alone?

How can you solve the problems of living alone after your spouse dies?

Of the seven kinds of retirement loneliness, the loneliness for a dead spouse is the most painful. Yet even that pain can be eased and eventually ended.

The best way to do it is to prepare for your spouse's death in advance. You know how to live alone together. Practice doing it. You'll build a life of your own with other friends. Since you're emotionally mature, they'll be real friends (see chapter 5). You can look to them for the tender loving care of feelings and touch that abolish loneliness.

Living alone together is a kind of loneliness insurance. It will not enable you to replace that special emotional rapport you had with your spouse, but it will give you the emotional support you need from others to continue with your life and make that life a happy one.

If your spouse should die and you haven't practiced living alone together and haven't made real friends of your own, you'll need to put your new antiloneliness attitude to work for you to make new friends. (In time, one of those friends could become your new spouse.)

But until that time comes, you'd be living by yourself. That means long hours without anyone near you. It's in those hours, in the quiet after you've made your evening meal and the night yawns ahead, that you're wide open to attacks of loneliness.

An attack of loneliness means you have an urgent desire to satisfy your two antiloneliness needs. You want loving, face-to-face emotional responses from someone. You want someone near you whom you can touch, and who will touch you, with love. You can't satisfy those two antiloneliness needs when you're alone. But you can come surprisingly close and nip each attack of loneliness in the bud when you adopt the second new emotionally mature attitude: During the time—especially the long nights—when I'm alone, I must draw on my own resources to satisfy my antiloneliness needs.

Here's how to put this second antiloneliness attitude to work for you.

GUIDELINES TO STOP ATTACKS OF LONELINESS WHEN YOU'RE ALL BY YOURSELF

The first three guidelines show you how to get into a good frame of mind even though you're living alone. That gives you the confidence to do something about your loneliness.

1. Enjoy your own company. Think. Dream. Plan. Weave fantasies. "Solitude . . . is the most blessed thing in the world," Helen Hayes said after her husband died. "The mind relaxes and thoughts begin to flow."

2. Do all the crazy things you've always wanted to do but couldn't because you were afraid somebody might catch you at it. That can often turn solitude into an adult playtime.

3. You're free—take advantage of it. You can plan things you want to do and do them, without consulting anybody. The cold fresh air of independence can be a bracing tonic.

The next two guidelines show you how to prepare to get satisfaction of your antiloneliness needs from others. Knowing that your preparations will enable you to satisfy those needs will tide you over during those periods when no one is around.

4. Use your solitude as a springboard for social contacts. Make a list of people you want to see and arrange to see them. Set up strategies for meeting new people—how, when, and where.

5. Think up ways of giving loving emotional responses to other people. It's easy. Just ask yourself how you like other people to give loving emotional responses to you. Words? Gestures? Embraces? When you know what you want, you have a better idea of what other people want.

The next two guidelines show you how to satisfy your first antiloneliness need—getting loving emotional responses from others—by getting those emotional responses from yourself.

6. Be your own companion, critic, adviser, and booster. When you like yourself, as you do if you are emotionally mature, you can become a real friend to yourself in your period of solitude. And a real friend supplies the loving emotional responses you need.

7. Invent projects that give you a lift. They can be practical (making a dress) or poetic (watching fleecy clouds scudding across the moon), but they must make you feel as wonderful as you want to feel at the time. Getting emotional satisfaction from the things you do is very much like getting loving emotional responses from another person.

Some people can get more emotional satisfaction from themselves than they can get from others. These are the kind of people who are self-sufficient. You probably know at least one person who you feel can get along without anybody. But if you're like most of us, you can't. To you, getting emotional satisfaction from yourself is not the same as getting emotional satisfaction from others. But it is the next best thing. And it's a great comfort when you're alone.

The next two guidelines show you how to satisfy your first antiloneliness need—getting loving emotional responses from others—by getting those emotional responses from people who are not with you.

8. Get the loving emotional responses you need from people you never met and never will meet. You know the loving emotional responses you'd like to hear from other people and see in other people. You can find those responses in books, paintings, sculpture, music, radio, TV, newspapers, and magazines. From these sources, build up a library and draw on it whenever you need it. Many people find just such comfort from the Bible; others find it in favorite books, poems, and symphonies.

9. Get the loving emotional responses you need from people you know while they're away from you. Write letters and make sure you're giving loving emotional responses in every letter you send out. You'll find the responses you're after in your mail box. Use the telephone the same way. (But be careful. This instrument can be a package of emotional dynamite. You never know, for example, what mood the person on the other end is going to be in. A bad telephone call could pitch you into a fit of loneliness and depression.)

The final guideline shows you how to satisfy your second antiloneliness need—touching, and being touched, with love—even though you're alone.

10. Make use of a "touch substitute." Nothing can replace skin-to-skin contact. But scientists will tell you that the human voice sends out vibrations that touch every part of your body. That's why lonely people often turn on their radio, TV, or stereo the moment they get into the house. A multimillion-dollar Dial-a-Voice industry (Dial-a-Prayer, Dial-a-

Joke, and so on) has sprung up to serve the lonely with the *feel* of a human voice.

But these touch substitutes go only one way—to you, not from you—and you need to touch as well as to be touched. Use the phone to establish voice contact. And use the cassette. Correspond with it. Your voice will touch your friends and people you want to be your friends. When your voice carries love, the voices coming back to you echo it. On a cassette, you can listen to that message over and over again when you're alone.

Follow these ten guidelines and you'll find that solitude will bring you not anxiety and terror but a durable calm. Then, alone, you'll be able to get to know yourself better than ever before. Aware of your powers to satisfy the emotional needs of others, you'll be able to build meaningful emotional linkages, real friendships, with more people. No more will you moan, "A part of me died when he [she] died." Instead, you'll shout to yourself joyfully, "I can survive emotionally by myself. I'm a whole person. I'm glad to be alive!"

When you're lonely when you're alone, you're in bad company. No emotionally mature older person need ever be.

Can you turn loneliness into happiness?

Loneliness can strike when you're with other people and when you're alone. In both cases, you can strike down loneliness by satisfying your two antiloneliness needs (the need for loving emotional responses from another human being and the need to touch, and be touched, with love). You do that by adopting two antiloneliness attitudes. Check to see that you've done so.

Have you adopted the two antiloneliness attitudes?

When you're with people, do you apply this antiloneliness attitude: I must give loving emotional responses to others to get loving emotional responses from them?

When you're alone, do you apply this antiloneliness attitude: During the time—especially the long nights—when I'm alone, I must draw on my own resources to satisfy my antiloneliness needs?

Happiness comes when you solve your retirement problems. When you apply these two emotionally mature attitudes, you have the ability to solve your problem of loneliness. You can turn loneliness into happiness.

Only when you're linked to others emotionally can you be happy. In the next chapter, I'll tell you how you can transform the closest linkage you can make with another human being into the most joyful, exhilarating, and overwhelming experience of your life.

# 11

Sex After Sixty-five

There *is* sex after sixty-five.
And after seventy-five.
And after eighty-five.
"Sexual activity is possible for at least a hundred years," says Harvard Medical School's Dr. Alexander Leaf.

What's more, 15 percent of men and women over sixty-five report a rise in their sexual output. And many women come to their first climax in later years.

These are the findings of recent studies made by internationally renowned sex researchers William H. Masters and Virginia E. Johnson and by Duke University's prestigious Center for the Study of Aging and Human Development.

In essential pleasurable responses, Masters and Johnson found no difference between younger and older men and women. Since the man becomes naturally capable of sustaining the sex act longer as he gets older, his pleasure and his partner's pleasure can be even greater than ever before. Realistically, some pleasures of sex do decline later in life. Intercourse is less frequent. It takes longer to become aroused. But up to about eighty, the rate of decline is so slow that many sexually active retirees fail to notice it.

These facts add up to this: You can continue to function as an interested and interesting sexual partner for as long as you live.

If you don't, it may not be your body that betrays you; it may be your emotions. Dr. Edward Adelson, a psychiatrist specializing in sex therapy in Florida's retirement belt, has found that 95 percent of all sex problems are psychological. He concludes that sex lasts as long as *you* want it to.

Why do one out of three men and women stop having sex when they get older?

They have been brainwashed by a myth. This myth says that if you are "older"

- you have no desire to make love
- you can't make love even if you want to
- you'll hurt yourself if you try to make love
- you're perverse if you even think about making love
- you're so physically unattractive that nobody would want to make love with you, anyway

You recognize the myth. You grew up with it. Sex, you probably believed in your youth, was only for the young and beautiful. What was virility at twenty-five was lechery at sixty-five. There was no such thing as a sexy senior citizen. Your parents went to bed together to sleep —period; it was difficult to imagine anything else.

If you've carried that sex myth over into your retirement, it's little wonder that you're one of the one out of three Americans over sixty-five who have decided "No more sex for me." You may even be embarrassed when others wander into your bedroom.

Why do seven out of ten men and women continue to have sex after sixty-five on a regular basis?

They enjoy it.

But they, too, might have been brainwashed by the sex myth, and enjoying it may make them feel guilty. Dr. Joseph T. Freeman, a specialist in the sexual aspects of aging, tells of a couple in their seventies who made love once a day yet believed that they were doing something unnatural. Their love-making seemed to them "an expression of some abnormal inclination."

Can you have sex later in life without guilt?

Yes, when you adopt this new emotionally mature retirement attitude: Sex at an older age is natural. It's moral. And it's one of life's greatest pleasures.

If you stopped having sex, can you start again?

Certainly. You can always rediscover sex. What's more, if you've never enjoyed it before (many of your generation, particularly women, have not), sex is "always there to be ... appreciated for the very first time," writes

Dr. R. N. Butler, expert on sex and aging, "whether you are young or very old."

Why should you start having sex once you've stopped?

The majority of retirees are finding sex increasingly pleasurable. Why be left out?

TEN REASONS TO CONTINUE TO HAVE SEX

---

1. You can enjoy sex physically as much as, or more than, before. Get rid of the notion that sexual enjoyment turns off after menopause. Actually, you could be turned on. The years immediately after change of life are described by playwright Tennessee Williams as "a second spring."

The term "change of life" used to imply neutering (becoming a member of neither sex), dwindling, the end. Now change of life means a change of renewal of a person's individuality.

2. Sex can help you stand up to ageist slurs. At a time in your life when ageists may depict you as feeble and sickly, senile and sexless, it's a wonderful feeling to prove to yourself that you're strong and healthy, alert and sexy. And to prove it regularly.

3. Sex makes you feel needed and wanted. That's an ego-boosting necessity at any age. In older years, when your ego may be under constant attack, it's more of a necessity than ever.

4. You can enjoy sex in privacy. The kids are gone, may have been for some time. You and your husband or wife can do what you please when you please. Many retirees are exploring the new excitements of daytime sex and sex outside the bedroom.

5. Sex can improve your health. "Sexual activity," claims Dr. Butler, "can be therapeutic for an older person."

6. Sex helps you stay younger longer. Stress, writes Dr. Hans Selye, the foremost authority on how the body grows old, ages one rapidly. Sex releases tensions and fights off stress.

When Dr. Edward Brecher, lecturer on Sex for the Mature Adult, was asked at a panel discussion if an active sex life keeps people young, he answered, "Sure. What do you think keeps this panel young?" Dr. Brecher looks fifty. He's close to seventy.

A man or woman actively involved in sex is motivated to stay attractive. That means exercise, diet, grooming, mental alertness, and emotional brightness.

7. You can make up for lost time. If you were brought up to believe sex was dirty, you felt ashamed of your sexual fantasies and suppressed them. Try to adopt a new sexual attitude: It's right to have sex, and anything I do sexually with a consenting partner is right.

Let yourself go. Dr. Sallie Schumacher, head of a sex therapy center at a leading New York hospital, was asked what she felt was not right between sex partners (of any age). She replied, "Nothing that both are agreeable to."

Many retirees have told me how angry they are that their early training deprived them of the joys of sex for most of their lives. "I'm furious," one woman in her sixties said. "If I had known all along I could do what I'm doing now, I could have had a great time. I feel cheated."

"What are you going to do about it?" I asked.

"Make up for lost time," she said.

Retirement is the time to make your dreams come true. Sex dreams, too.

8. Sex can add zest to your life twenty-four hours a day, every day. Sex doesn't begin and end in bed. It goes on continually in glances, twinkling eyes, caresses, kisses, fondlings, and the lilt in your voice. Sex means chatting about nothing and everything, recalling rose-colored days, murmuring secrets to each other, laughing together, whispering your fears, your uncertainties, playing pranks, teasing. Sex is fitting your bodies together in sleep like two pieces of a jigsaw puzzle. When sex is a promise, all contacts become sensual and stimulating, and life together takes on a heightened zest.

As you grow older, sex is not an overriding obsession as it often is in youth; your eyes aren't filled with stars, and skyrockets don't go zoom in your heart. But sex can brighten all the things you do with your spouse. One woman in her sixties made this sober assessment of the role of sex in her married life: "It's like adding a fine sauce to fine food."

If you're one of the many retirees who suffer from twenty-four-hour-a-day-togetherness boredom, sex could be a remedy.

9. Sex is an affirmation of love. Does your husband or wife love you after all these years? What older person hasn't felt that nagging doubt? Sex cries loud and clear, "Yes, I love you." It banishes doubts. It gives you the love security you can't do without.

When love is affirmed, companionship, understanding, and mutual respect grow. There's an open exchange of feelings (remember those wonderful, warm intimate talks after sex?) that brings you closer together. What's more, being sure you're loved brings with it a sense of belonging, of inner serenity, of self-esteem, and of being special.

This next is the key reason.

10. You can raise sex to a new peak emotional experience. Love between a man and a woman in older years is different than at any other time of life and more precious. For the emotionally mature retiree, it's

- accepting the other's uniqueness
- adjusting willingly to the other's emotional deficiencies
- understanding the other's emotional needs
- responding instantly to the other's emotional needs each time they're revealed by the language of emotions
- giving of oneself completely to satisfy the emotional needs of the other

It's the warmest and most enduring emotional linkage between two human beings.

It cannot exist in youth because the surge of sex's biological demands clouds and confuses the emotions. It cannot exist in middle age because the many roles you're forced to play can mask your true emotions. Only in older years can you completely know each other emotionally and satisfy each other emotionally. Only in older years are you completely free to love and be loved.

Without love, sex is cold and mechanical. You'll come away from it disconsolate, depressed, and empty. But come to it with love, and, for possibly the first time in your life, your longing for the satisfaction of your deepest emotional needs and your desire to touch, and be touched, lovingly will be gratified together. It's an emotional experience that could peak above all others in your life.

Why does sex sometimes go sour even in emotionally mature retirement marriages?

You may enter retirement with a hang-up about sex that you must get rid of before you can put your new sexual attitude to work for you. You may feel that learning about sex at your age is unnecessary, indecent, and embarrassing. So you go into the same stale act (how many years has it been since you've tried anything new?), and you watch your desires slowly expire from boredom.

Get rid of your hang-up by realizing that sex manuals are now respectable. They're approved by medical, religious, and mental health groups. Why not get started by asking your librarian to recommend a book for you? (Truly, he or she won't bat an eyelash.) It could open a whole new world of sexual excitement to you—and to your partner. The whole joy of sex, advises psychiatrist Dr. Domenick A. Barbara, is to find your partner's needs and satisfy them. The same rule applies to sex as it does to emotions: Satisfy your partner's needs and he or she will satisfy yours.

Make use of the varied techniques of sex (and don't think you can't master them now as easily as you could in your youth—you can), add love, and you'll come away from the sex act rewarded, refreshed, and eager for more.

Many retirees are frightened of impotence or frigidity—or of just not being able to perform up to their mate's standards. So, rather than face rejection, they give up. If you're one of those retirees, applying the right sex techniques could prove your fears groundless. Early retirement may under some conditions be desirable, but early retirement from sex never is.

You're over sixty-five, widowed or divorced. Should you marry again for sex?

Not entirely for sex. But sex (with love) could be a top priority consideration.

Yet the idea of sex-love marriages for older people still meets with condemnation from many younger people. Dominated by the sex myth described earlier, they can't understand sexual attraction between older people. To them, marriage between older people is acceptable only when the bride and the groom declare it's for companionship, to share interests, to dispel loneliness, to have somebody to take care of, or to achieve financial security.

Good reasons all. But no retirement marriage can succeed without the closeness that comes from love. And sex is the affirmation of love. Sex and love are the roots of a happy retirement marriage. The almost eight out of ten retirees who marry happily are driven by the sex-love urge, no matter what socially acceptable reasons they're forced to give in public.

But times are changing. Writer Jacqueline Low reports that many elderly no longer claim they marry for companionship and that some women in their sixties and seventies even discover sexual love for the first time in their lives.

And a study conducted for the National Institute of Mental Health by Barbara Vinick shows that there is much more awareness that older people can have sexual interest—and that it's usual.

But whether your children will share this new attitude of sexual enlightenment toward older people when you announce your intention to marry for love and sex is questionable. If they blow up a storm, and they may, put to work all you've learned about communicating with younger people (see chapter 7). Explain your new emotionally mature retirement attitude about sex: It's normal, it's virtuous, and it's beautiful.

Then add, "I realize love and sex are not all of marriage. I know the character of the person I'm going to marry, and it's a fine one. I know we won't have to worry about money or health any more than anybody else does at our age. And I also know that at our age, we have a better chance to make our marriage work than you would if you remarried at your age." Tell them why.

"We have none of the pressures of middle-aged marriage—no children to bring up, no careers to worry about, no keeping up with the Joneses. We have only one goal in life—to make each other happy. We know there isn't as much time, so we'll work very hard at it. And that kind of hard work is a delight."

Should you have sex without marriage?

Uncle Sam gives many older men and women no choice—it's either sex without marriage or no sex at all. Here's what's behind this shocking fact.

The Social Security laws in most cases cut off a widow's or a widower's benefits upon remarriage. But a couple can live together without marriage, and their checks will continue to roll in. Stephen Loudon, a Social Security Administration official, estimates that each year at least eighteen thousand men and women begin to live in "Social Security sin." "That's about two thousand more older people," he adds, "than get married."

Sex without marriage is now a trend among older people. Should you follow it? Start to arrive at your decision by answering these key questions yes or no.

FIND OUT IF YOU'RE READY FOR UNMARRIED SEX
---

1. Have you found a sexually desirable person whom you love and who loves you?
2. Is marriage impractical (for any reason)?
3. Do you want the freedom to call the whole thing off in case things go wrong—with no strings attached?

Answer yes to question 1 and yes to either question 2 or 3, and you're ready.

Then come to your final decision by applying your new emotionally mature attitude toward sex: Sex at an older age is natural. It's moral. And it's one of life's greatest pleasures.

Add another new emotionally mature retirement attitude you've already adopted (see chapter 9): Do it now!

If you think you'll have opposition from your children when you consider remarrying, imagine the flak you'll get when you tell them you're going to live with a member of the opposite sex. In one extreme case, children tried to have their elderly mother committed to a mental institution because she had moved in with her lover. (They failed.) If you make a decision for sexual liberation, tell your children frankly why you're doing it. When they understand, they'll be on your side.

Can you live together unmarried without affecting the moral standards of your grandchildren?

No. That's why some retirees who find it impractical

to marry enter into a "cohabitational contract." In lieu of a civil or religious ceremony, the contract is signed in the presence of friends and relatives. It's the moral equivalent of a marriage, and when the grandchildren ask, "Is Grandma married?" their parents can answer yes. In this way, the legally unmarried retirees preserve the tradition of marriage for their grandchildren.

Is it difficult to find a sexual or marriage partner when you're older?

It can be if you're a woman. In the over-sixty-five age bracket, there are five unmarried females for every unmarried male. What's more, one out of every two males in that bracket who remarry wed females younger than sixty-five. Those figures add up to the possibility that ten women of about your age may be going after the same eligible man. You've got to learn how to stand out.

You're an unmarried woman over sixty-five. How can you find a partner?

By putting two emotionally mature attitudes to work for you. One you may have always had. The other is a new emotionally mature retirement attitude.

Dr. S. Walton Kirk, a clinical psychologist, says that throughout our lives we search for and sell our best features to gain the world's approval. He advises people to just continue to sell their best.

The first attitude: Sell your best.

But before you can sell your best, you must bring out the best in you. Here's how to do it.

WORKING ON PHYSICAL ATTRACTIVENESS

Older women in Europe do it all the time, and many are quite stunning. Deplorably, that's not so generally true in the United States. Our garment and cosmetic industries cater almost exclusively to the young. There's only a handful of places that specialize in beauty care for older women (and they're in big cities and are expensive). A survey conducted for this book found only one of the nation's top corporations offering a session on "female grooming in retirement" in their preretirement training programs. If you want to bring out your best, chances are, you'll have to do it yourself.

To help you, here are some hints from a New York beauty and fashion consultant who specializes in helping older women look their best.

Stay away from old-fashioned styles. In particular, avoid bouffant hairdos, red shoes and green shoes, and matching shoes, hat, and bag. They date you.

Stay with the times. Do your preliminary shopping in the pages of the better fashion magazines (*Harper's Bazaar, Vogue*). Then go out and buy yourself some "now" clothes. (Don't look in the half sizes if you've been accustomed to looking there. Those sizes include some very unflattering garments. Pick out full sizes in styles and colors a stylish middle-aged woman would be proud to flaunt, and have them altered to fit you.) No trick to it, and you'll be astonished by the transformation. You'll look fashionable and up-to-the-minute. A person will be able to see at a glance that you're living in today's world and not in the past.

Stay with the look of less. By current standards, the more natural you look, the better you look. Any newsstand beauty magazine will cue you in on popular products and techniques. Experiment with makeup in front of your mirror until you come up with the kind of soft natural look that suits you best. Don't use harsh blue or green eye shadow—that is, unless you want to put on ten years in the blink of an eye.

Clothes and cosmetics, though, can only accentuate your basic attractiveness; you have to be attractive to start with. And these days, there's no reason why you shouldn't be. Your public library shelves are packed with easy-to-follow guides on how to slim down and shape up. Pay attention to your hair, your skin, your posture, and your teeth.

And remember, when you look attractive, you feel attractive. That will give you the confidence to go after the man you want.

WORKING ON EMOTIONAL ATTRACTIVENESS

As an emotionally mature older woman, you know how to solve retirement problems. What man won't find you emotionally attractive when you help him solve his? When you feel a man needs and wants your help, give it.

Keep your mind and heart open to the language of emotions. When you read the emotional needs of the person you want to be with, satisfy them. Sympathy and understanding are among the best qualities you can have.

Emotional attractiveness lights up your eyes, brightens your features, and makes you glow with vitality.

Now that you've brought out the best in yourself, take action. You can't if you're still hung up on the old-fashioned attitude that females should be demure and passive and must wait for the males to take the initiative. If you wait at your time of life, you could wait forever. Instead, adopt this new emotionally mature retirement attitude: In sex and love, a woman can be as aggressive as a man—or more so.

So go out and be aggressive. Where? Wherever the pickings are good. At lectures, in the supermarket, at political meetings, in your apartment-building elevator, at parties, while walking down the street. "If I see a man about my age who appeals to me," a feisty sixty-three-year-old woman boasted, "I just stop him and say hello. Sure, I get rebuffed sometimes. So what? I just bounce back. Who knows, some day I may hit the jackpot!"

There's no reason to get butterflies in the stomach about how to portray your best. You've worked at bringing it out, haven't you? It's made you into a new you. But that new you *is* you. So, just be yourself. There's no sounder way to attract a man and keep him.

Although the statistics favor men in this situation, they, too, must be physically and emotionally attractive. All the hints for women can be applied to men.

Sex in older years can be part of your life. Add love, and it can be the emotional experience of a lifetime. For the rest of your life.

You're no longer ashamed of feeling the sex drive. But there are other emotions you're still ashamed of having in retirement. That leaves you a potential victim of the crime of emotional blackmail. What is it? You'll find the answer in the next chapter. And you'll also find how you can make that crime pay off for you.

12

Emotional Blackmail Against Older People

Pat Nichols is a sixty-six-year-old widow. She's self-supporting and lives in Akron, Ohio. Her son is a successful disc jockey in a southern Florida city, and his wife is a writer for a local public relations agency. They have two small children and a large house. Recently, her son called her.

"Look," he said. "We can't have careers without your help. We want you to come down here and run the house and take care of the kids."

At sixty-six, Pat Nichols has decided to leave the city in which she has spent all her life and shoulder the burdens of raising another family. She shudders at the task ahead of her. "But what was I to do?" she says hopelessly.

Her son grins and tells his friends, "Now I'll be free as a bird."

He's a successful emotional blackmailer.

There are hundreds of thousands like him preying on older people.

Emotional blackmail isn't legally a crime; it's morally one. But while only an extremely small number of older people are victimized by muggings and other much publicized crimes (less than a quarter of one percent, according to some figures), emotional blackmail is likely to strike almost every person of retirement age at one time or another. The sufferings caused by it are intense and long-lasting. On the long list of crimes against older people, emotional blackmail is number one.

Just what is emotional blackmail?

Let's take the case of Pat Nichols and play detective. We know who the criminal is. Let's find the crime.

"Mrs. Nichols, what would have happened if you had said no to your son?"

"He would have said a lot of things I didn't want to hear."

"Such as?"

" 'You owe it to me, Ma. Do you remember the time I wanted to go to music school, and you wouldn't let me? So you owe me this.' "

"You felt guilty?"

"Not only about the music school, but about, oh, so many things I did wrong for him."

"And you didn't want him to bring your guilt feelings out into the open?"

"He would have, you know, if I hadn't said yes."

Without putting it into words, her son had threatened her. The unspoken warning was "I'll expose the guilt you feel toward me unless you pay off by becoming my housekeeper and a substitute mother to my kids."

That's emotional blackmail—payment extorted to prevent the disclosure of an emotion you're ashamed to have exposed.

Besides feeling guilty toward your children, do you have other emotions you're ashamed to have exposed?

When you were growing up, you might have been given three guidelines for social approval—be useful, have friends, be loved. You've always been ashamed to feel useless, lonely, loveless. When these emotions take hold, you hide them from others.

When you hide your shameful emotions from others, how does the emotional blackmailer know about them?

You never can hide them completely. They leak out in telltale actions. The astute emotional blackmailer recognizes them. You may not be aware that they're giving you away, but they are.

Discover what some of your telltale actions are by answering yes or no to the following questions. You'll find out what your answers mean at the end of the questionnaire.

ARE YOU VULNERABLE TO EMOTIONAL BLACKMAIL?
---

1. Do you give your grandchildren gifts (from dolls to tuition) of things your children wanted but you never gave them?

2. Do you tell your children how well you've provided for them in your will?

3. Do you volunteer to help your neighbors with their laundry, shopping, house repairs, and other things, which you never would have done when you were working or raising a family, even though you had the time?

4. Even though you don't like volunteer work, do you sign up, anyway?

5. When you don't hear from your children for two or three days in a row, do you call?

6. Have you become a "joiner" since you retired?

7. Do you hint to friends that you'd like invitations from them?

8. Do you make slighting remarks about your husband or wife when you're with others?

9. In company, do you laugh extra loud at ageist sex jokes? For example, Bob Hope is asked, "Is there sex after sixty-five?" He answers, "You bet. And awfully good, too." [Pause.] "Especially the one in the fall."

10. When your husband talks freely to others, do you make comments such as "No wonder he's talking so much—he never opens his mouth at home"? If you're the husband, do you make similar remarks about your wife?

Here's what your answers mean.

Any yes answer means you're vulnerable to emotional blackmail. The more yeses you checked off, the more vulnerable you are.

Each yes indicates you've taken an action that reveals a hidden emotion.

If you answered yes to questions 1 or 2, you are *feeling quilty toward your children.* A yes answer to question 3 or 4 reveals you are *feeling useless.* Yes to 5, 6, or 7 says you are *feeling lonely;* and if you answered yes to questions 8, 9, or 10, you are *feeling unloved*.

Read over each question. Your answer states your action. Read what your answer reveals. That's the way your emotional blackmailer reads you.

Why are you more vulnerable to emotional blackmail in retirement than at any other time of life?

There are four reasons.

You're more likely to feel guilty toward your children. They've grown up but perhaps not quite the way you wanted them to. Whose fault is it? Yours, you feel.

You're more likely to feel useless. You've given up your job. Forever. Your children have left. They won't come back. What's there to do? Nothing, you feel.

You're more likely to feel lonely. One by one, you may be losing contact with everybody you know. And you don't know how to make new contacts. Who's there to turn to? Nobody, you feel.

You're more likely to feel unloved. A barrier of silence may separate you and your spouse. Your built-in sexual taboos may push you farther apart. What's happened to love in your life? It's gone, you feel.

Who are the emotional blackmailers?

Your children. Your friends. Your relatives. Your husband or wife. Volunteer organizations.

Who are the most vicious emotional blackmailers?

Your children. Only they can threaten to expose all four of the emotions you're ashamed of. Take the case of Pat Nichols again. She thought her son would haxe exposed her guilt feelings toward him if she had refused to pay off. But he could also have exposed her other hidden emotions.

"Ma, I don't understand you. How can you not come? You don't have a thing to do. Don't you want to feel useful for a change?"

Or

"Oh, come on, Ma. We all know how lonely you are. You haven't a friend in the world. Come on down, and you'll have a ball with the kids."

Or

"Ma, Ma, Ma. Since Dad died, you could use a little loving. Where are you gonna find it—in that little apartment of yours all by yourself? This is retirement country. You never know who you'll meet down here. Change your mind."

These speeches sound well meaning, but they're deadly. Rather than hear them, Pat Nichols would have done anything her blackmailer demanded. Most retirees would have done the same.

Who are the crudest emotional blackmailers?

Your friends, relatives, wife, or husband. Some cases follow.

"Clara, the girls are coming over for coffee on Tuesday. We all want you to come. And don't forget to bring those wonderful pies and cakes."

Clara will have to spend a day and twenty dollars or more (a lot of money when you're on Social Security) to bake for twelve women. But she'd rather pay off than say no and hear her friend snort, "Well, if I were as lonely as you seem to be, I'd do anything to be with people."

"Stanley, Mother wants to go downtown shopping. Will you get in your car and come over and pick her up?" "Stanley, come on over and set up the chairs and tables for tomorrow's party." "Stanley, you've got a power saw, haven't you? Look, I want to put up some bookshelves in the kids' rooms. Why don't you come over and put some elbow grease behind that saw and save me a job?"

Stanley always agrees, though he'd much rather use his retirement leisure in more pleasant ways. He's not going to say no and risk having one of his relatives sneer at him, "You mean you've got something useful to do instead? Well, that's a surprise!"

"Fred, as long as you've got the time now, let's visit Shirley and Alex."

Fred hates Shirley and Alex. But he'll go. And he'll do a lot of other things with his wife he refused to do before his retirement. He doesn't dare say no and take the chance she'll snap. "We don't talk together. We don't have sex together. At least, we can do some things together." He doesn't want to hear that love has gone out of his marriage.

Who are the most subtle emotional blackmailers?

Volunteer organizations.

Their recruiting is high-minded. "Help other people" is the pitch. Nothing could be nobler. There isn't the remotest hint of blackmail.

But if you turn them down?

Your children, friends, and relatives do the hatchet job on you. That's what the volunteer organizations rely on (they call it the pressure of public opinion). Just listen.

"What's the matter with you—you have so many friends, you don't need any more?" "You've finally got a chance to do something useful, and you refuse?" "You're so happy living alone, you don't want to meet somebody you may like?"

Retirees know that if they don't join, they'll hear that they're lonely, useless, and loveless. They don't want to hear it. They join.

But they don't admit they've been blackmailed. "I joined," they say, "because I've always wanted to help other people. Now I have the time." They keep the secret of their shameful emotions. And volunteer organizations keep the up-to-$25,000 a year they would have had to pay had the older workers been salaried employees.

Do emotional blackmailers realize what they're doing?

Some do (like Mrs. Nichols's son). Some don't. They read the victim's weaknesses intuitively and take advantage of them intuitively. But whether the emotional blackmailers realize what they're doing or not, the result is the same—you pay off.

What kind of payoffs do emotional blackmailers demand besides services?

Money is one thing.

Emotional involvement is another. "I have this acquaintance. She called and said, 'I've just had an awful blowout with my son. He wants to marry again, and I think the girl is a mess. I've just got to have somebody to talk to. I'm coming right over.' I don't want to get involved. It's a terrible drain on me. But if I had told her not to come over, she would have said, 'What else have you got to do?' Who wants to hear you feel useless?"

Can you stop emotional blackmail by admitting your shameful emotions?

Of course. If there's nothing to be exposed, you can't be blackmailed.

But bringing your shameful emotions out into the open takes guts. You have to say to your children, "I feel guilty for so many things I didn't do for you." You have to admit to everybody you know, "I feel useless, lonely, loveless." Most of us just can't do it.

Even if you're able to do it, that won't stop people from victimizing you. They'll simply take advantage of the weaknesses you've revealed. Like so.

"Mom and Dad, listen. I've got this tip on a stock. It's going to double in a week. I know how guilty you feel about some of the things you said no to in the past, so let's wipe the slate clean. All I need is a few thousand dollars."

No guilt feelings *if* you pay off. You pay off.

"Ma, I know how lonely you are. Come and stay with us for a few weeks. And, oh, while you're here, you won't mind baby-sitting, will you?"

No loneliness for a few weeks *if* you pay off. You pay off.

"Phil, I know you feel you're on the shelf. I've got this cellar I want to clean out. Got this bad back. Thought you'd be pleased as punch to pitch in."

No feeling of uselessness for a while *if* you pay off. You pay off.

"You know, honey, if we just could get away by ourselves for a while, things could be different. Bermuda—a cruise. It won't cost that much, and, honey, it could make so much difference."

A holiday from feeling unloved *if* you pay off. You pay off.

The name of the crime has changed, that's all. It's no longer emotional blackmail. It's emotional extortion.

How can you stop the emotional blackmailer?

Stop feeling guilty toward your children. Stop feeling useless. Stop feeling lonely. Stop feeling loveless. You can do it when you put your emotional maturity to work for you in ways you've already learned.

You can stop feeling guilty toward your children when you realize that in retirement you have no responsibility to do anything about your old failures (see chapter 2). The past is past. In retirement, you start with a clean slate.

You can stop feeling useless when you believe that in retirement you have the right to do anything with your free time—including nothing—as long as it gives you pleasure (see chapter 6). What you do, or don't do, may not look "useful" to other people, but it's useful to you. And that's what counts.

You can stop feeling lonely when you give of yourself to satisfy the emotional needs of others (see chapter 10). Then other people will satisfy your emotional needs. And that's how real friendships are made. When alone, be your own best friend.

You can stop feeling loveless when you know what love is in later years and how to show it (see chapter 11). When you give love, love will come to you. Or come back to you.

When you've freed yourself of these four emotional weaknesses, the emotional blackmailer can't strike. Neither can the emotional extortionist.

Nobody will be able to blackmail you again into joining a volunteer organization. If you want to join, you'll be able to do so—voluntarily.

How can you profit from emotional blackmail when you're the victim?

First, realize that you are being emotionally blackmailed.

That's hard. You don't want to know that people you trust, even your children, are exploiting you. You put it out of your mind.

But you're being hurt. Take a look at your situation. You're chaining yourself to projects you don't like and don't want. You're handing over money you need. You're tying yourself up in emotional entanglements that couldn't concern you less. Doesn't that make you want to see red?

Well, see red. Get angry. Get hopping mad!

Your negative emotions are surfacing and that means you have a problem (see chapter 4). If you want to stop those negative emotions from eating away at your well-being, face up to your problem: You are being emotionally blackmailed. Then put your negative emotions to work for you by getting started on making a decision to solve your problem.

You know what decision to make. Apply the right emotionally mature retirement attitudes (they've been pinpointed for you under the previous question). And when you do, you'll reap the profits.

You'll no longer feel guilty toward your children. You'll no longer feel useless. You'll no longer feel lonely. You'll no longer feel loveless.

And that's just the beginning.

Make little speeches.

"Look, kids, you don't realize it, but every time you've asked for a check, you've been playing on my guilt feelings. Well, I don't have any anymore. So you're not going to get as many checks. From now on, every request will be reviewed strictly on its merits."

Or, to your friends and relatives,

"I've been glad to help out in the past. I'm sure you asked me to do it because you thought I was lonely or I wanted something to do. Well, I'm not lonely, and what I do—or don't do—is just fine with me. So don't ask me to fetch and carry. From now on, that's one of the things I don't do."

Or, to your wife or husband,

"I've tried to hold this marriage together, done all the crazy things you wanted me to do, because I didn't have the guts to admit this wasn't a marriage at all!. But now I know how to make it a marriage, with love. Wait and see. In a little while, you won't want to push me into doing things I don't want to do."

Those little speeches can make you feel like a giant. But don't chalk that up as profit yet. There is a danger.

When you tell your blackmailers off, you could lose them—your children, your friends, your relatives, your spouse. It's a risk you must take.

As a practical matter, though, it's not much of a risk. Your children may sulk and clamp a telephone boycott on you, but it won't last long. Your friends, relatives, and spouse may wail, "I've never been so hurt in my life!" and go into a stew, but they'll come round. It's a thousand to one shot that you'll lose anybody.

And when you take up with them again, it will be on a new basis. They'll admire and respect you. It's a good start to true friendship and love. Add that as a profit, too.

Emotional blackmail is not new. You might have been one of its victims without realizing it. What is new is that now for the first time, you can recognize the crime. You can stop it. And you can make it pay off for you—in money, time, and emotional energy saved. And, more important, in a restored sense of dignity and in happier relations with the people close to you.

Feeling useless is an emotion you're ashamed of. But when you're retired by your place of business even though you want to go on working, that emotion is thrust on you. Yet, it's only one of the emotional hazards of mandatory retirement. In the following chapter, you'll find out what the others are and how you can use them to create a happy life in retirement.

13

The Shock of Mandatory Retirement

A shock is an emotional hammer blow that can have a devastating effect on your health. According to the National Center for Career Life Planning, of the forty major shocks that can batter you from infancy through old age, the shock of mandatory retirement ranks ninth, just behind deaths of members of your family and divorce.

"[What frequently happens] during the first four months after retirement," reports psychologist Ira J. Tanner, "is ... that there is a likelihood of heart attacks and strokes—all related to the trauma [mandatory-retirement shock]."

In the opinion of some researchers, the end of work is the start of physical and mental decline.

Mandatory-retirement shock can be as debilitating to you as loneliness or the fear of death. And as deadly.

What is mandatory retirement?

It's a fancy name for being fired when you reach a

certain age. You may want to continue to work, you may be capable of doing your job—but you have no choice. As soon as the computer spots you're at retirement age, you're out.

What is the mandatory retirement age?

It varies. For New York fire fighters, it's fifty-five. For air traffic controllers, fifty-six. For Harvard University professors, seventy. For most people, it was sixty-five until recently.

In 1978, a federal law raised the mandatory retirement age to seventy. This may have little or no effect on the normal retirement age. Big corporations may try to induce their employees to retire before seventy (preferably no later than sixty-five), since the lower retirement age means substantial dollar savings for the corporations. When a worker retires at sixty-five rather than at seventy, the corporation saves five years of payments to the pension fund. The corporation also is able to replace the higher-salaried older worker with a lower-salaried younger worker five years sooner. Unions, too, are likely to urge retirement no later than sixty-five, since they have come to regard early retirement as a fringe benefit. Employees themselves may be disinclined to work past sixty-five. (Before the passage of the new law, the mandatory retirement age at General Motors was sixty-eight, but on the average, only two out of ten thousand workers stayed until then. Most GM workers called it quits at sixty-five.) Moreover, there are loopholes in the new law through which some employees can still be forced to retire at sixty-five. The chances are good that sixty-five will continue to be regarded as the usual retirement age.

How did sixty-five come to be regarded as the normal retirement age?

This was the result of an arbitrary decision of Congress. In 1935, the Social Security Act fixed sixty-five as the minimum age at which an employee could retire and collect benefits. Congress didn't make any scientific study before it picked sixty-five; it was very much like pulling a number out of a hat. But once the Social Security Act was passed, everybody assumed sixty-five was the normal retirement age.

Before the passage of the Social Security Act, when did people retire?

They didn't. Most people worked until they died or were physically unable to continue.

Did the Social Security Act introduce the concept of retirement?

On a mass scale, yes. The act guaranteed the right of almost any employee to retire. And it backed up that right with a government subsidy.

That means the concept of retirement for all is only a little more than forty years old. If you're in your sixties now, you were in your twenties when the Social Security Act became law. That makes you a member of the first adult generation in the United States to live in a society in which retirement is a way of life.

Does the Social Security Act force you to retire?

No. You can work as long as you like provided you're willing to give up some, or all, of your benefits, which normally begin with retirement at age sixty-five. After seventy-two, you can work and still collect benefits for the rest of your life.

The Social Security Act is responsible for retirement, but don't blame it for mandatory retirement.

Is ageism to blame for mandatory retirement?

Not at all. Put the blame on World War II and greed. Mostly greed. Here's the story.

While World War II was being waged, Uncle Sam froze wages and clamped down hard on excess profits. Corporation executives invented a way to collect more, anyway. They simply deferred extra income (which was illegal) until after they had retired (which was legal). The gimmick was called the pension.

It was hijacked virtually overnight by the giant unions and delivered to their millions of blue-collar workers. The pension became as American as Mom's apple pie.

But there's a drawback to pensions, which nobody wanted to notice in the rush to rake in the chips. The annual amount your corporation pays into a pension fund for your pension increases with your age. By the time you reach age X, that amount has grown so large that your cost to the company is far more than you can earn for the company. You're a liability, and you've got to go. The pension, which was invented to get you more, gets you fired.

Age X is your mandatory retirement age. It's not fixed by age discrimination. It's fixed by your pension cost.

Is every employee in the United States subject to mandatory retirement?

No. Pension funds cover only half of the work force. That means one out of two working men and women are computerized to retire at age X. (The number of non-pension-funded companies practicing mandatory retirement is negligible.)

Each year, about sixty thousand men and women in this country are forced to retire at age X, which, up to now, has been overwhelmingly sixty-five. How many are victims of mandatory-retirement shock?

No one knows. This emotional disease is so new that statistical teams have not yet tackled the field. One thing is certain, though—if you were forced to retire, you could have become a victim of mandatory-retirement shock. And if you're not yet one, you still could be.

Doesn't mandatory-retirement shock strike only during the first four months of retirement?

No, it doesn't. It could strike several months, a year, or several years after you retire.

Some retirees are protected from mandatory-retirement shock by the excitement of relocation, travel, or new activities in the period immediately following retirement. When the effect of these new experiences wears off, mandatory-retirement shock strikes.

Can it strike you, even though you have been happily retired for years? Find out for yourself by answering the following questionnaire. (It's just as valuable to you if you're not yet retired.) Read each question and choose the answer under column A or column B that most closely represents your feelings. (Or if you're not yet retired, rephrase the questions in the present tense. For example, question 1 will then read, "On the whole, *do* you regard your fellow workers...?"

CAN MANDATORY-RETIREMENT SHOCK STRIKE YOU?

	A	B
1. On the whole, did you regard your fellow workers, on and off the job, as	great people?	nothing special?
2. On a scale of 0 to 10, would you have assessed your value to the company you worked for as	over 5?	5 or under?
3. When you spoke of your job, did others listen with	respect?	indifference?

	A	B
4. When new acquaintances asked, "What do you do?" did your answer make you feel	good?	embarrassed?
5. On Sundays and holidays, did you feel very	lost?	free?
6. If your job had strongly influenced how and where you lived, who your friends were, even what choices were open to you in your spare time, would you have found that	desirable?	all wrong?
7. If you had been called a company man or company woman, would you have been	pleased?	outraged?

Here's what your score means.

If you chose all seven answers from column B, you're immune from mandatory-retirement shock.

If you picked up to three answers in column B, mandatory-retirement shock can strike you but not dangerously so.

If you selected four or more answers in column A,

mandatory-retirement shock can hit you hard. The more answers you chose in column A, the harder you can be hit.

If you chose all seven answers in column A, mandatory-retirement shock could strike with shattering force.

What causes mandatory-retirement shock?

Dr. Abraham Monk, a professor of social work, has found that many workers consider work as a good in itself, a basic part of life without which the rest has little meaning, that living and doing are the same thing.

The implication is clear. Without work, life isn't worthwhile. "When one goes off duty forever," one researcher observes, "there is a sense in which one becomes ... dead." And it's that feeling that is thought to be the cause of the shock that has such terrifying effects on your mind and body.

But do employees really equate work with life itself? Ask typical preretirees what they think about losing their jobs at retirement age, as one of my researchers has done, and the chances are ten to one they'll tell you that they will be glad to get rid of the job stresses, office politics, pressure from younger workers, boredom, fatigue, monotony, or various other things. That doesn't make work sound like something you can't live without. Life, it would seem, only starts when work stops.

Here's a fresh look at the problem.

It's not the loss of work itself that causes mandatory-retirement shock. It's the loss of the emotional satisfactions that your job gives you. There are seven such satisfactions.

SEVEN EMOTIONAL SATISFACTIONS
YOU LOSE WHEN YOU LOSE YOUR JOB

1. You lose the satisfaction of feeling close to your fellow workers. This creates a kind of loneliness. You can't get rid of it by visiting with your old buddies again. They've taken on new loads. The place has changed. They share inside jokes, grievances, and interests with one another. You no longer speak their language; they're deaf to yours. You feel out of it. There's no way back in.

2. You lose the satisfaction of feeling useful to your company. Once you've been let go, your mind may be teeming with ideas, your skills may be as sharp as ever, and you may have more experience than anybody there, but your company may not want any part of you. You feel you're not good for anything.

3. You lose the satisfaction of feeling respected. In our society, holding a steady job (almost any job) brings respect from others. When you're out of work, you're down and out in other people's eyes.

4. You lose the satisfaction of feeling you're a somebody. When people meet you for the first time, they ask, "What do you do?"

You answer, "I'm a teacher," or "I'm a steam fitter," or "I'm a reporter," or "I'm a truck driver," and so on. You get a feeling of importance from identifying yourself with what you do—you're a somebody. If when you're jobless and are asked what you do, you answer, "Nothing," you feel like a nobody. You feel like nothing.

**5. You lose the satisfaction of feeling you have somewhere to go and something to do every work-

ing day, on schedule. Your job routine gives a sense of order to your life. You know what to expect. You feel safe. Shatter your job routine and you never know what the next minute will bring. You feel threatened. You face each day anxious and uneasy.

6. You lose the satisfaction of feeling the pattern of your life away from your job has been planned for you. Your job establishes that pattern in three indirect ways.

- Your job determines where you live; and that means who your neighbors will be, and possibly what kind of community life you'll lead.
- Your job determines how much money you have to spend, and that means the kind of life-style you'll lead.
- Your job determines who works with you, and that means perhaps who many of your friends will be, and what you'll do after working hours when you're with them.

"With a job," one retiree commented wistfully, "you know what to do on the job—and off."

But without a job, you have to decide where you'll live, how you'll live, and who your friends will be. You have to build a whole new pattern of off-the-job life for yourself. And you don't know how to do it. You feel lost and confused. Your life is in a state of chaos.

7. You lose the satisfaction of feeling you're being taken care of. The company you work for picks up many of your medical bills, pays for time off for vacation, may provide recreational facilities for you and your family, maps out your day, plans for your future, and signs your paychecks. What's expected of you in return is loyalty.

Mandatory-retirement shock is not a single blow but the blows of seven separate emotional losses. Not every retiree experiences every loss, though a good many do. The greater the number of losses you experience, the more intense the shock.

Is job satisfaction different from the seven kinds of emotional satisfaction you get from a job?

Yes. Job satisfaction means emotional satisfaction from the actual work you perform on the job. For those who derive pleasure from actually performing their work, job satisfaction should be added to the list of emotional losses caused by mandatory retirement. But many Americans find their actual work drab and frustrating. Many retirees never had job satisfaction, so they don't regard it as a loss.

Are the emotional satisfactions you get from a job lost only when you're forced to retire?

No. They're lost any time you're fired. At any age.

Then why didn't you experience something like mandatory-retirement shock when you lost your job earlier in life?

Because you knew there was another job out there waiting for you. What you'd lost, you'd regain. This confidence in the job market softened the blows of your emotional losses. Losing your job was a shock, but you never went to pieces. What is different this time is the feeling that you'll never work again. A retiree told Dr. Monk, "It's the end of the road. No matter how useful we've been, nobody needs us any longer. We're done." That special group of emotional satisfactions you can get only from a job may be gone forever. There is a sense of irreplaceable loss of something very dear to you.

Can you fight off mandatory-retirement shock by getting another job?

You can.

But it must be real work. A retired college professor pleads, "I need to work. Not make-work, not a hobby, not volunteer work—I need a job." Only another job can replace the emotional satisfactions you lost when you lost your job.

But at sixty-five, a job is hard to get. "A worker who loses a job after sixty," warns a bulletin from the Social Security Administration, "may never work again." We are, adds nationally syndicated financial columnist Sylvia Porter, "consigning productive older Americans to human garbage heaps." Mandatory retirement may not be ageism, but mandatory unemployment after retirement is.

How can you protect yourself against mandatory-retirement shock when you can't get another job?

Make up for the emotional satisfactions you lost with similar feelings that give you as much, or more, satisfaction. You can do that with emotional maturity, with the guidelines and attitudes you've already learned about in this book.

HOW TO PROTECT YOURSELF AGAINST MANDATORY-RETIREMENT SHOCK
---

1. **Make up for the loss of feeling close to your fellow workers with a feeling of real friendship for other people.** To make a real friend, give of yourself (see chapter 10).

2. **Make up for the loss of feeling useful to your company with a feeling of being useful to yourself.** To feel useful to yourself, decide what gives you pleasure and go after it (see chapter 6).

3. **Make up for the loss of feeling respected because you have a job with a feeling of being respected for yourself.** To earn respect, work at being a distinct individual (see chapter 5).

4. **Make up for the loss of feeling you're a somebody because of your job with a feeling that you're a somebody because of the kind of person you are.** To be a somebody, work at keeping your mind sharp and improve yourself (see chapter 5). The way you see it, it's not what you do that counts but what kind of person you are.

5. **Make up for the loss of the feeling that you have somewhere to go and something to do according to company schedule with a feeling that you can set any schedule you please.** To set up your own schedule, just do what comes naturally. You could find you're scheduling doing nothing and liking it (see chapter 6).

6. **Make up for the loss of feeling that the pattern of your life away from your job has been planned for you with a feeling that you can plan your own life.** To plan your own life, commit yourself to making decisions (see chapter 4). That always makes your life richer and more exciting.

7. **Make up for the loss of feeling that your company takes care of you with a feeling that you can take care of yourself.** To take care of yourself, become emotionally mature for retirement (see chapters 2, 3, and 4).

How can you turn mandatory-retirement shock to your advantage?

Protect yourself against it. When you do, you turn every loss into a gain. Read over the seven ways to protect yourself against retirement shock, and you'll see

1. You lose your relationship with your fellow workers. But you gain true friends.

2. You lose your usefulness to your company. But you gain usefulness to yourself.

3. You lose the respect you got because you held a job. But you gain respect for yourself as a person like no other person in the world.

4. You lose the good feeling you got from identifying yourself with your job. But you gain the good feeling you get from identifying yourself as a superior human being.

5. You lose workdays scheduled for you. But you gain leisure days you schedule for yourself.

6. You lose a life away from work that's been planned for you. But you gain the chance to plan a better life for yourself.

7. You lose the security your company gave you. But you gain the ability to rely on yourself. And that's a feeling that makes you feel ten feet tall.

Your gains far outweigh your losses.

A somber note. You might have gotten emotional satisfaction from the actual work you did before retirement, but you may never get that satisfaction from the same work during retirement. You may never be doing the same work.

But here's encouragement. Make all seven ways to prevent mandatory-retirement shock work for you, and you'll gain the self-esteem and self-assurance you need to get started on your own on some other activity. It needn't be related to anything you did before as long as you get emotional satisfaction from actually doing it. (I was the president of a college before retirement; now I lecture and write books and articles about the emotional aspects of retirement. It's nothing like the administrative work I did at the college. I loved that work, but I get a bigger kick out of what I'm doing now.)

Can voluntary retirement produce a shock?

Yes, and it can often be just as severe as mandatory-retirement shock. This happens after the novelty of retirement wears off and the sense of irreplaceable emotional losses sets in. Protect yourself against voluntary-retirement shock the same way that you do against mandatory-retirement shock.

The only way you can be free of the threat of retirement shock, voluntary or mandatory, is to approach retirement without any emotional attachment to your job (that is to say, when you circle no answers in column A of the questionnaire in this chapter). But I don't know of anybody who does.

Mandatory retirement is being legislated out of existence in some communities, and this may be the start of a national trend. Will this end mandatory-retirement shock?

Where there's no mandatory retirement, there can't be mandatory-retirement shock. But in those communities where mandatory retirement has been outlawed, 50 percent of the employees choose to retire, anyway (even where retirement benefits are substandard). And every man and woman in that 50 percent is a candidate for voluntary-retirement shock.

In this chapter, I've shown you how to protect yourself against mandatory-retirement shock and turn it to your advantage. You can do the same for voluntary-retirement shock. It takes work because you have to do it yourself. In the next chapter, I'll tell you how more than a million retirees are buying a way of life that effortlessly may protect them from either kind of retirement shock.

14

The Retirement Community—Paradise or Purgatory?

How would you like to have your home (you pick the size and style) in a beautifully landscaped rural community that offers you the following features?

- two championship golf courses
- a well-equipped pro shop
- a golf-cart port built onto your home
- twelve tennis courts
- sixteen handball courts
- several dozen shuffleboard areas
- bicycle paths
- woodland walks for hunting with a camera
- a twelve-lane bowling alley
- twenty-four Ping-Pong tables
- boating and fishing in six lakes
- three swimming pools
- gourmet dining (plus a flock of snack bars)
- festive balls
- top-name live entertainment

- current movies
- a community cable-TV station (plus network TV)
- a community newspaper
- a library
- twelve churches of various denominations and a synagogue
- no municipal, state, or inheritance taxes
- no taxes on food or medicine
- living costs about 25 percent less than elsewhere in the state
- two banks
- a full-time fire department
- twenty-four-hour complete protection by a fully manned sheriff's department (nobody locks doors or bicycles)
- a complete 100-bed modern hospital
- fourteen general practitioners and a team of medical specialists
- three dentists and an optometrist
- free bus service at fifteen-minute intervals
- an amateur theatrical society
- a fine arts league
- dozens of hobby groups (with free instructions)
- more than 100 clubs
- a group of men and women who bicycle about the community spreading warmth and good cheer (and who are known, appropriately, as cycle mates)

What's more, the pollen count is among the lowest in the nation, and the temperature is a balmy seventy-four degrees (average) all year round.

Paradise? It could be a purgatory.

It's a retirement community.

What are the most likely conditions for living in a retirement community?

There could be several. You may have to resign yourself to living the rest of your life exclusively with people of your age group or older; visits by young people are usually not encouraged, and in many retirement communities, small children are verboten. You may also have to be willing to give up the outside world. Most of the goods and services you need from the outside are channeled through your retirement-community management, so you can live a life free of significant contact with outsiders. You contribute nothing to the outside world.

Consenting to make working at play a way of life is another possible condition. In a retirement community, fun and games are scheduled like work assignments; and you work as hard at them as you ever did at your job. And finally, being able to pick up the tab is an important factor.

Can you afford to live in a retirement community?

The community described in the opening section of this chapter is one of the most luxurious in the nation, yet you can buy a home in it for less than $20,000—an eye-popping low in today's inflated real estate market. Other homes in the community go for up to $100,000. The average price is $50,000. Community banks finance up to 80 percent of your cost. And once you've settled in, you and your spouse can live for as little as $500 a month, including mortgage payments.

Retirement communities are built so that retirees can afford them.

Do the people who live in retirement communities like the life?

Dr. Kenneth Paul Berg is the nation's ranking authority on retirement communities; he founded sixty-seven church-affiliated ones himself. A survey he conducted indicates that 98 percent of retirement-community dwellers find wholesome satisfaction and an active, interesting, enjoyable life. These people were enjoying their retirement by doing things they never had time to do when they were busy raising families.

When he asked caustic, probing questions, such as, "How can you say you like living in an old-age ghetto?" or "Do you really enjoy living in a playpen for the elderly?" he was answered with, "Don't knock it until you try it."

At one leading retirement community, he found the retirees to be the most enthusiastic group of any age he had ever seen in his life.

How popular are retirement communities?

The first retirement community—Sun City, a sprawling complex near Phoenix, Arizona—went up in 1960. There are now more than 300 retirement communities, located in just about every state of the union, including Alaska. More than one million people live in them; and by 1996, Dr. Berg projects, that number will have soared to more than five million.

So popular are retirement communities that one business writer advises younger people to "put your money into real estate development companies that are building retirement communities so that at retirement you'll have enough cash to buy a better home in one of them."

Why are retirement communities so popular?

The advertising copywriters for the retirement communities have an answer.

"Where would you rather live? In a hostile world that's put you on the shelf? Or in a friendly community that guarantees you a dynamic new way of life? Make the swap and you'll gain far more than you lose."

Here are some of the gains you can expect. The examples read like typical advertising testimonials.

"I enjoy being with people my own age. Imagine what stares a grown man would get riding a tricycle down a city street. Here, everybody thinks it's normal."

"When we take a rare trip away to areas where there are small children, what a relief it is to come back to peace and quiet!"

"I can relax and enjoy myself. For the first time in my life, I don't have to worry about a thing."

"All I want to do for the rest of my life is have a good time. And where can I have a better time than in a retirement community?"

"When you can see a couple out walking at ten, eleven, or even after midnight, holding hands, just out for a walk, that's security. I couldn't get that feeling of safety back in the city if I had paid a quarter of a million for a Park Avenue co-op."

But do these advertised gains really outweigh what you lose when you give up the world you lived in for your whole life? Judge for yourself. Assume that you're thinking about entering a retirement community. On a separate sheet of paper, write down the number under the appropriate column for each question. Add the numbers to determine your loss and your gain.

HOW TO DECIDE WHETHER YOU GAIN OR LOSE WHEN YOU ENTER A RETIREMENT COMMUNITY

How do you value what you lose?

	Not Important	Important	Vital
1. The stimulation you get from living with people of all ages is	1	5	10
2. Close contact with your family is	1	5	10
3. A chance to participate in a world where things are happening is	1	5	10
4. A chance to still do meaningful and creative work is	1	5	10

	Not Important	Important	Vital
5. The dozens of small familiar things of everyday life that gave you comfort and happiness over the years are	1	5	10

How do you value what you gain?

	Not Important	Important	Vital
1. Living with only older people is	1	5	10
2. Freedom from noisy children, including your own grandchildren, is	1	5	10
3. Putting your welfare in the good hands of retirement-community management is	1	5	10
4. Living in a world where every day is a holiday is	1	5	10

	Not Important	Important	Vital
5. The personal safety of yourself and your spouse is	1	5	10

Compare your gain with your loss. Chances are, your loss will outbalance your gain and possibly by a large margin. But if you're like the 50,000 or more retirees who'll buy into a retirement community this year, you'll sign up anyway. That's because you know instinctively that what the ads sell is just the frosting on the cake and that your real gain is something more important: The retirement community protects you against most of the emotional hazards of growing older.

And that's the reason why retirement communities are so popular.

Retirement shock (mandatory or voluntary) is an emotional hazard of growing older. Does the retirement community protect you against it?

Yes.

How?

By giving you the same seven emotional satisfactions you get from a job. (The feeling that these satisfactions are lost forever triggers retirement shock.)

CLOSENESS TO YOUR "FELLOW WORKERS"

They're the other retirement-community members who work at play with you. (Virtually all retirement-community activities are carried out in groups, even reading.)

USEFULNESS TO YOUR "COMPANY"

Your "company" is the retirement community. You give pleasure to others by working at play with them. Pleasure is the business of the retirement community, and you help produce it.

RESPECT FROM OTHERS

In a retirement community, working at having fun, no matter what kind of fun, earns you the respect of others. Decide to sit around and do nothing, and you're treated like a bum.

SELF-RESPECT

When you're asked, "What do you do?" you answer, "I play golf," or "I'm in a dance group," or "I play shuffleboard," or "I act," and so on. You get a feeling of importance from identifying yourself with the activity you work at most. You're a somebody. (Inside the retirement community, as on the outside, you are what you do.)

A JOB ROUTINE

You leave your home each morning and go to activities according to a timetable set for you by the retirement community. (In the posh retirement communities, people come home after a hard day's work having fun and relax with a night on the town.)

A PATTERN TO LIVING

Once you've determined where you'll live in the retirement community, the community determines how you'll live, who your friends will be, and what options are open to you when you're not working at play.

SECURITY

The retirement community looks after your pleasure, your health, your safety, and your general welfare. And it packs the empty hours of your day with fun things to do. You feel as coddled as a pampered child and just as secure.

The retirement community may give you a better chance at "job" satisfaction than ever before. The only way to get emotional satisfaction from the actual work you do is to like the work. And when is work likable? When it's fun. It's as if the retirement community had given you a new job—the job of having fun. And as long as you have a job, you're immune to retirement shock.

A word about "working at play."

If you're like most retirees, you've lived your life according to the work ethic. That's the belief that work gives you dignity, a sense of worth in your own eyes and in the eyes of others. How, then, can you retain your dignity in retirement when there is no work? One way—turn fun into work.

But working at play isn't easy (unless you're a compulsive golfer). It needs organization, grit, and discipline. Doing it day in and day out is as tough as staying on a diet. You won't work at play unless you're forced to. And here's where the retirement community comes in. It forces you to.

And do you work! Retirement-community watcher Thomas Meehan writes, "This writer, who is still almost a quarter of a century away from retirement age, is exhausted at merely having to list the seven-days-a-week, morning-to-night goings-on."

What do you work at?

"Golf, bridge, dancing, a musical extravaganza, gymnastics, badminton, needlework," answers a retired newspaper editor. "The folks here [in the retirement community in which he lives] really work at play. They share experiences in the stamp club, the walking club, the film and slide club, or with fellow painters or craftspeople. It's an active bunch."

Working at play is not a retreat into second childhood. It's a way of retaining your dignity in a society dominated by the work ethic. When you do a good job of working at play, you become a respected and admired member of your community.

The sex myth described earlier is also an emotional hazard of getting older. Does the retirement community protect you against it, too?

Yes. The myth is effective only in a youth-oriented society. It loses its power once you cross the border into a society where everyone is older. Many couples, reports Thomas Meehan, happily renew long-suspended sex immediately upon getting into their retirement homes. What's more, you stop feeling perverse and guilty when you indulge in sex, even when the sex is extramarital. "More hanky-panky goes on," observes Meehan, "than the outside world would ever believe."

The retirement community is where the sexual revolution of older people is happening.

What other emotional hazards does the retirement community protect you against?

There are many.

AGEISM

In a community where only older people exist, ageism can't.

YOUNG PEOPLE

There aren't any. (And the few who visit are treated like a minority.)

LONELINESS

A sense of belonging to the community substitutes for the lack of emotional linkages with other human beings that you might feel if you didn't live in the community.

DECISIONS

Retirement is the age of decision, but the retirement community makes all the major ones for you.

MOST OF THE FIFTEEN KEY RETIREMENT PROBLEM AREAS OF EVERYDAY LIFE

Hobbies, finding a job, feeling safe, deciding what to do with your free time, selecting a home, and so on, cease to be retirement problem areas in a retirement community.

Since the retirement community protects you against most of the emotional hazards of old age, how can it possibly be a purgatory?

If you're an emotionally mature retiree, you can protect yourself. You don't need the retirement community to protect you.

Then what's left for you inside the community?

A low-cost safe life in pleasant surroundings with easy access to a complex of recreational facilities.

That's a plus. A big one.

But there are some minuses that come with it.

· You want to express the real you. But you must conform.

· You want to be free. But your life is laid out for you.

· You want to explore all the potential you've unlocked inside yourself. But you're locked into a life very much like the social life of your middle years, every day, night and day.

· You want to be an individual. But you're molded into a typical retirement-community member.

· You want to rely on yourself. But you have no choice except dependency.

· You want to be part of the world. But you're shut out from it.

· You want to tell other community members how you feel. But they can't understand your emotionally mature attitudes.

If you're like 15 percent of the retirees who buy into a retirement community, you'll weigh that big plus against your minuses, and you'll get out within a year. You'll have spent nearly a year in an emotional purgatory.

However, according to Dr. Berg, of those who remain, 98 percent find the retirement community a paradise.

If you're a retirement-community member, you get respect and admiration you never would get in the real world. If you're an emotionally mature retiree, it's only in the real world that you look for respect and admiration. In the next chapter, I'll show you how to get both in your community.

15

How to Gain Respect in an Ageist Community

Older people have not always been targets of ageism. In New England meetinghouses in colonial times, the seats of honor went to the older participants, even when they were paupers. Young people were taught to regard the elderly with respect bordering on awe. So great was the authority and dignity of age that men, and women, too, actually tried to make themselves look older.

Older people dominated our society and continued to do so until about a hundred years ago. Then, as the nation struck out into the unexplored West and blazed new paths in science and industry, we began to turn to the young for leadership. The older people were too set in their ways to meet the challenge of frontiers. They knew little of the new worlds opening up around them. "I have yet to hear the first syllable of valuable or even earnest advice from my seniors," accused youth-revolt spokesman Henry David Thoreau. "They have told me nothing, and . . . they cannot teach me anything." The older generation was holding back progress, and the nation wanted no part of it.

But it wasn't until a little more than forty years ago that this feeling of separateness from the older members of society started to take on concrete forms. In 1935, the passage of the Social Security Act made older people officially separate, though it gave them financial consideration. In 1940, the code name *senior citizen* (it has a negative connotation) made its first appearance. In the sixties, the youth cult, spearheaded by Elvis Presley and JFK, thrust the older generations out of the mainstream of American culture. Within your lifetime, older people became almost aliens in their own land.

Ageism is that new.

How do the ageists justify their prejudice?

The same way racists justify theirs—their standards for acceptance just aren't met.

What are the ageists' standards for acceptance?

You must be a valuable human being. By a "valuable human being," ageists mean themselves—as they would like to be. The same standards they set for themselves (and more often than not achieve), they set for you. Here they are.

1. You must be a distinct individual. This is the most important standard.

You must also

    2. work for your keep
    3. fit in with your fellow workers
    4. get along without demanding special privileges

5. build toward a better future
6. lead a normal sex life
7. contribute to the community's prosperity

Are virtually all younger people ageists?

Yes. You were one yourself until you retired. Again, if you have retired early, you face many of the same problems that those who retire at sixty-five, seventy, or older face. Face it: It's the older members of the community against the rest of the community—and the rest of the community is the overwhelming majority.

Since ageists are an overwhelming majority, do they determine the community's standards for acceptance?

They do. So from now on, I'll refer to the ageists' standards as the community's standards.

Is it true that many older people do not meet their community's standards for acceptance?

Yes. Many retirees feel it's impossible to maintain these standards, and they don't even try.

If you're like these people, here's how you fail to meet the most important standard. You don't continue to be a distinct individual. You let down and become an older person like all other older persons. You begin to look shabby and old-fashioned, as if you were falling to pieces.

No matter where you are or what you're doing, you seem to be in a rocking chair, dozing. (You've seen "typical" old persons on TV, particularly in commercials. Don't they all look alike? talk alike? act alike? What you see on TV you can see in your mirror.)

And here's how you fail to meet the other six standards.

You don't work for your keep. The ageists feel your attitude is "I've worked hard all my life; the world owes me a living." The community sees you as a parasite, even if you are living on your savings and/or private pension. Or, if you do work, you don't fit in with your fellow workers. You either go all out and make them look bad or you're so out of it that they have to work harder to make up for your inefficiency. The community sees you as a troublemaker.

You don't get along without demanding special privileges. You insist on them—that people put themselves out for you, be concerned about your welfare, visit you, fuss over you, pay you homage. Why? Because you're older. That attitude makes no sense to the young. The community sees you as a cranky nuisance.

You don't build toward a better future because you don't believe you have any future. You live in the past (that's all you talk about). The community sees you as a living fossil.

You don't have a sex life. Your attitude (and theirs) is: Sex ends in the older years. The community regards a normal sex life as the sign of a normal human being. The community sees you as a freak.

You don't contribute to the community's prosperity. You don't work, and with your family gone and your income slashed, you're a poor consumer. You're no longer a member of the middle-aged groups that make things happen. What's more, the moment you slip your senior citizen's identification into your wallet or purse, you become a card-carrying outsider. You withdraw from the world while living in it. You're of no help to the community, but the community now has the moral (and often legal) responsibility to help you. The community sees you as a social problem.

When you fail to live up to the community's standard of individuality, you become a stereotyped older person in appearance and manner. This is the *physical* image you project to the community (see chapter 5).

When you fail to live up to the community's six other standards for acceptance, you become a stereotyped older person in the way you behave in critical life situations. This is the *psychological* image you project to the community.

Your physical and psychological images together make up your portrait as your community sees it.

What does the portrait of you that your community sees look like?

You've just seen it piecemeal. Now view it in its entirety.

They see you as

- an old-fashioned has-been, no different from millions of other old-fashioned has-beens
- a parasite
- a troublemaker
- a cranky nuisance
- a living fossil
- a freak
- a social problem

Like what you see?

Ageists might have painted your portrait. But you can redesign it—when you live up to your community's standards for acceptance.

How can you gain the respect of your community?

By meeting your community's most important standard for acceptance: Continue to be a distinct individual.

It's easy to let down and become the stereotyped physical image of an older person, particularly when it's expected of you. So you must make up your mind to work at being a distinct individual. Be guided by that emotionally mature retirement attitude (see details in chapter 5), and you'll be yourself in the way you look, the way you talk, the way you move, and in everything about you. You'll stand out in a crowd. And that earns respect—at any age.

Here's a success story.

"I found myself shuffling," one retiree told me. "It was comfortable. I admit it. It didn't take much effort, and I kind of liked it. But then I saw I was shuffling like all the other older men. I didn't like what I saw. I didn't want to be like them. So I decided I would work at not shuffling. With every step I took, I said to myself, 'Do not shuffle. Do not shuffle,' and I made an effort not to. It wasn't easy. It took a long time. But you know something? I don't shuffle anymore."

I've seen him walk. He's in his seventies, and he has the stride of an athlete. More important—it's his own distinctive stride.

Here's a better success story.

This retiree worked on her physical image from the

day she retired. She never let down. At seventy-five, she looks no more like the "typical" older person than a movie star looks like an extra.

And here's one tragic story.

A famous actress (you've seen her in old films on TV dozens of times) found the temptation to let down after sixty-five too strong. At the age of sixty-seven, she was a guest at a Hollywood premiere. When pictures from the event appeared in the newspapers, she took one look at herself, saw a typical older person, and declared, "I'm never going out in public again." She never did.

To be a distinct individual in older years, you must work at beating back the temptations not to be.

How can you gain the admiration of your community?

Meet any of the other six standards (numbers two through seven) of acceptance set by the community, and you'll get respect. The more of these standards you meet, the more respect you'll get. Meet all six standards, and in addition to great respect, you'll get admiration. Reason? Nobody thinks you, or any other older person, can do it.

But you can.

Here are six steps to follow.

STEP ONE: WORKING FOR YOUR KEEP

"It's unfair," one retiree told me, "to set that kind of standard. They throw me out of work, they make it impossible for me to get work, and then they treat me like a second-class citizen because I don't work."

Sure, it's unfair. But what are you going to do—sit around and moan and complain? That's just what they expect you to do. Instead, be guided by this emotionally mature retirement attitude (you're familiar with it from chapter 6): If I can live on my retirement income, I need work that gives me job satisfaction. If I can't live on my income, I need work that earns me money whether it gives me job satisfaction or not.

The key word is *need*. When you let this attitude take over, you will realize you need work, and you won't be satisfied to sit on your hands. You'll go out and look for a job. And if no job is available? Then you'll make work for yourself—work that can pay off as well as, or even better than, a job. Here are some ways to do it.

You've probably thought about this idea yourself.

Go into business. That takes money. But some businesses take little money. Others can be financed with government loans. Call your local Small Business Administration office. They'll surely help you with advice and possibly with cash.

And here's a new idea.

Free-lance your talents. Let's say you're a retired housewife ("retired" because you're no longer bringing up a family). You know how to take care of children and run a household. Why not put an ad such as the following one in your local paper?

> I'll House Sit or Baby Sit
> Experienced, reliable woman will run your house, take care of your children for a day, a week, or as long as you like. Pets love me. Reasonable rates. Call 123–4567.

Everybody has talents. Are you a good mechanic? Can you play the harmonica at parties? Do your recipes make people drool? Run ads, pick up your telephone, write letters, slip handbills under doors—tell people what you have to offer, and you'll be surprised at the offers you'll get.

The point is not to think about work only as holding a regular job or running a business. Both of those kinds of work may be closed to you. But you can always free-lance.

And here's the newest idea.

Teach. Did you ever sit back and think you have a lifetime of skills and experience stored away in your head? Do you realize how valuable you could be to a child or a teen-ager—teaching them all the useful things you've learned? So why not do it?

The best way to get started is to sit down and write out a description of what you know and what you can do (remember, homemaking skills are as important as any other kind of skills). Send it to the heads of your local schools. Afraid you'll get a curt go-peddle-your-papers note in return? Don't be. A researcher for this book wrote such a description to a top executive of a prestigious New York private school, and this is the answer he received: "Thank you for your proposal. I will be very glad to discuss it with you. I am in my office on Monday and Wednesday afternoons from 4:00 to 5:00; no appointment necessary."

Education expert Gene I. Maeroff writes: "Retired people are being brought into elementary and secondary schools to tutor and share experiences with the young."

The doors to a new career in teaching are open. Walk in.

You will also earn the respect of the community by

going back to school or college to train yourself for a new job. More and more retirees are doing just that. Courses for retirement-aged students in colleges and universities have multiplied twenty-five times in the last five years (in many states tuition costs you very little or nothing at all). And if you're like most retirees who return to the campus, you'll make an excellent student. Your younger classmates may even honor you with a special name—OWL, which stands for *O*lder *W*iser *L*earner. (And don't forget, the secondary and vocational schools in your community would be glad to have you, too.)

Often, however, instead of being a preparation for work, education for retired people becomes a substitute for work. Retirees may work at learning as an end in itself and go on doing so for the rest of their lives. It's a trend, and it's become so pronounced that one private school is constructing a retirement community on its campus with classrooms replacing playrooms. Working at learning is more fashionable than working at play, but it can be almost as valueless when judged by the standards of your community.

Volunteer work does not generate the same amount of respect from the community as a paying job. The standard is that you must work for your keep. When you don't bring home a paycheck, you get no respect.

A clarification. Actually, there are degrees of respect. You do get some respect for the sacrifices you make when you contribute services. But on the whole, the attitude of your community is: If you could hold a paying job, you wouldn't have to work for nothing. If you get a top rating of 10 on your community's respect meter for holding a better job than you had before retirement, you'd get a rating of 4 for holding a volunteer job.

Other work substitutes rate lower than 10 as well. And so do some kinds of work.

HOW WORK AND WORK SUBSTITUTES RATE ON YOUR COMMUNITY'S RESPECT METER

Work or Work Substitute	Respect Rating
Holding a better job than you had before retirement	10
Running your own business	9+
Holding the same kind of job that you had before retirement	9
Teaching your own skills and experience	8+
Free-lancing your special talents	8
Attending school or college to prepare for a job	7+
Holding any job you can get	6
Doing volunteer work	4
Attending school or college as an end in itself	3

Work or Work Substitute	Respect Rating
Engaging in cultural activities (attending opera and ballet, visiting museums, and so on)	2
Working at play	1
Doing nothing	0

You can talk about getting the respect of your community when your respect rating is greater than 5.

A caution. Don't confuse respect with envy. An overworked employee may envy your working at play or doing nothing, but he or she may not respect you for it.

As an emotionally mature retiree, you're guided by the attitude that you can do anything you want with your free time, including nothing—as long as what you do gives you pleasure. And when you do what you want to do, you gain self-respect (see chapters 2 and 6). So why must you work?

Look at it this way. You have two choices.

When you choose to do what you want to do, and you don't work, you gain self-respect, but you lose the respect of your community.

When you choose to do what you want to do, and you do work, you gain self-respect and the respect of your community.

Pick one.

(My personal choice? I admire the retiree who does what he or she wants to do without caring for the respect of the community. But how many retirees can do it?

Can you? I know I can't. As long as the community makes adherence to the work ethic a requirement for respect, I'll work.)

STEP TWO: FITTING IN WITH YOUR FELLOW WORKERS

The secret is to communicate with them. They're younger, so that's a problem. But you know how to solve it (see chapter 7). Just explain your attitudes.

If they think you're an eager beaver, point out that all you want to do is a good job; you don't want to make them look bad. Then promise them you'll work up to their top standards and not set higher standards of your own. You'll still satisfy your desire to do a sound job, and you'll satisfy their desire for security.

If they think you're an old fogy, tell them you realize that tools and techniques have changed and that you're willing to start learning all over again. Then promise them that while you're adjusting, you'll work twice as hard so you'll be no burden to them. You'll earn their goodwill, and that will make it easier for you to earn your living.

In a while, the gap between you and your fellow workers will close. They'll treat you the same way that they treat one another. When you make a mistake, they'll let you know it. When you come through in the clutch, you'll get a pat on the back. You'll be one of them.

STEP THREE: GETTING ALONG WITHOUT DEMANDING SPECIAL PRIVILEGES

As an emotionally mature retiree, you know how to solve your retirement problems (see chapter 4). You know how to get what you want from yourself, from other people, and from life itself (see chapters 5 and 6). You can get along on your own without any help from anybody. You don't need special privileges, and you think it's demeaning to ask for them.

"I just want to be treated like everybody else," asserts one sixty-nine-year-old woman. "No better. No worse."

And that's the way you will be treated when you, too, assert that emotionally mature retirement attitude.

STEP FOUR: BUILDING TOWARD A BETTER FUTURE

At sixty-five, if you're a man, you can expect to live at least sixteen more years. If you're a woman, nineteen. What's more, the longer you live, the better your chances for living still longer. If you live to eighty-one, you can expect to live to eighty-seven. If you live to eighty-seven, you can expect to live to ninety-two. And so on. This year, Social Security payments are going to more than seven thousand men and women over a hundred. Take care of yourself, and you could live well into your nineties —or longer.

If you retire at age sixty-five, you have at least twenty-five years to live from the day you retire. And that's a dismally long time to go without goals. Goals are necessary for a vigorous life. Having goals means working toward them; every day brims with projects. It's these projects that give you the feeling of being involved, being in the world, and doing something important. They bring excitement to your life. They make you feel alive. In her acclaimed study of aging, *The Coming of Age*, Simone de Beauvoir observes, "The greatest good fortune, even greater than health, for the old person, is to have his world inhabited by projects: then, busy and useful . . . his oldness passes . . . unnoticed."

How do you find your retirement goals?

First, realize that you can't live in the past or relive

the past (see chapter 2). The goals of your earlier years are dead. You must find new goals.

Uncover the real you that was buried by the middle-aged roles you were forced to play (see chapter 3). Now you know what you want out of life, what you really want. Those are the goals of your retirement years.

When you build toward a better future, you gain something so many older people have lost forever—hope.

STEP FIVE: LEADING A NORMAL SEX LIFE

This is one community standard that you may find easier to meet, because you know sex can be a peak emotional experience (see chapter 11).

Don't worry about whether the community will know you're having a normal sex life. You don't have to advertise it. They'll know every time you walk down the street hand in hand with your spouse.

When the community regards you as a normal member, you won't feel that terrible sense of being pushed out. You'll feel you can take part in all the community's activities because you belong.

STEP SIX: CONTRIBUTING TO YOUR COMMUNITY'S PROSPERITY

You do when you work, when you pay property taxes for schools, when you spend your money in the community, or when you save in local banks. But that's only part of it. Do more.

Get involved in community affairs. Join consumer groups or political clubs. Write letters to editors.

But don't make the mistake of putting your weight only behind activities in favor of your age group. Be guided by this emotionally mature retirement attitude: I must work for the good of the whole community, not just for the good of my age group.

When the whole community benefits, so does your age group. It's an attitude that makes sense to all age groups.

When you meet all your community's standards for acceptance, you get respect and admiration at sixty-five, seventy-five, eighty-five—and at ninety plus.

To get the respect and admiration of your community, you've rejected the ageist stereotype. You're an emotionally mature retiree leading the kind of life that's best for you. What's that life going to be like? In the last chapter, I'll show you.

16

How to Predict Your Own Future

During retirement, certain emotional events can occur. They are the events around which your life will revolve. You can't escape some of them. How you react to them will determine the course of the rest of your life.

What are these pivotal emotional events of your retirement life?

There are eight that may occur.

1. The loss of your job
2. The loss of income
3. The loss of happiness in marriage
4. The loss of family unity
5. The loss of the respect of your community
6. The loss of looking middle-aged
7. The loss of your spouse
8. The loss of your middle-aged way of life

Each loss is devastating.

How can you react to these retirement losses?

You can react as an emotionally immature retiree and face a future of frightening possibilities.

Or, you can react as an emotionally mature retiree and make a good life for yourself.

Or, you can react as an emotionally mature retiree and transform your age into a triumph.

How is it that as an emotionally mature retiree, you can convert age into either a good life or a triumph?

The emotional events of your retirement life are problems. As an emotionally mature retiree, you know how to solve problems and have the ability to solve them. But problems have more than one solution. For each emotional event, you can choose a solution that leads to a good life or a solution that leads to a triumphant one.

What determines whether you choose a good solution or a triumphant one?

For any problem, you will choose the solution that gives the most emotional satisfaction. But what gives you the most emotional satisfaction changes with the stage of emotional maturity you have achieved.

In the first stage of emotional maturity, you get emotional satisfaction from a good solution.

In the second stage of emotional maturity, you find that you get emotional satisfaction only from a triumphant solution.

How do you grow in emotional maturity during retirement?

By solving retirement problems. The more problems you solve, the higher your degree of emotional maturity. Or, viewed another way, the more involved you are in living successfully *in* the world, the more emotionally mature you become.

Let's say you've achieved a high degree of emotional maturity. You can come up with triumphant reactions to the emotional events of your retirement life. Since you know what those events may be, you can predict what your reactions will be. Just choose your reactions to the following problems.

The first pivotal emotional event is the loss of your job.

YOUR REACTION

1. Bemoan the injustice of mandatory retirement and settle down to an old age of boredom and inactivity.
2. Live without a job by drawing on yourself for emotional satisfactions similar to those your job gave you and do anything you like, including nothing.
3. Get a job (a real job, not a job substitute); and if you can't get one, make a job for yourself (like going into a business, free-lancing your talents, or teaching your special experience and know-how).

EVALUATION OF YOUR CHOICE

Reaction 1 is an emotionally immature reaction; 2, a

good emotionally mature reaction; 3, a triumphant emotionally mature reaction.

TWO POINTS OF CLARIFICATION

The first point is that the idea that retirement is a reward, a time for pure enjoyment, may be a hoax. It was invented to justify mandatory retirement. Believe in that idea and choose to play for the rest of your life, and you'll lose the respect of your community (yes, the same community that promised you Fun Town, USA, after retirement). There's nothing wrong with rewarding yourself with a life of leisure; if that's what you want, it can be a good life. But you can't lead the best possible life—the triumphant life—without the respect of your community. And you can't earn that respect without going back to work.

The second point is that in middle age, your job was the focal point of your life. In triumphant retirement, it's one part of your life—and seldom the most important part (particularly when you work part-time). With that attitude, you put higher values on the other things you've always wanted to do—so you *do* them in your free time.

The second pivotal emotional event is the loss of income.

YOUR REACTION

1. Feel that the government owes you a living and join groups to lobby for increased benefits.

2. Forget about keeping up with the Joneses and live on your income by buying only those things that make you and your spouse happy.

3. Go out and earn more money (remember, you can make your own job if you can't find one).

EVALUATION OF YOUR CHOICE

Reaction 1 is an emotionally immature reaction; 2, a good emotionally mature reaction; 3, a triumphant emotionally mature reaction.

A POINT OF CLARIFICATION

For most retirees, investments are not the answer to loss of income. Because of inflation, when you invest a dollar, the dollar you get back can be worth less than the original dollar you invested.

The only way to maintain your buying power is to bring in dollars that will buy one dollar's worth of merchandise each. And the only way to do it is to work for them.

The third pivotal emotional event is the loss of happiness in marriage.

YOUR REACTION

1. Accept it as a fact of old age and live with it.
2. Separate or divorce.
3. Bring happiness back into your marriage by understanding the emotional needs of your spouse and adjusting to them and by convincing your spouse to do the same for you.

EVALUATION OF YOUR CHOICE

Reaction 1 is an emotionally immature reaction; 2, a good emotionally mature reaction; 3, a triumphant emotionally mature reaction.

A POINT OF CLARIFICATION

Separation or divorce is an emotionally mature solution only when you've explored your real "me" and your spouse's real "me" (see chapter 8) and concluded that your spouse cannot satisfy enough of your emotional needs. If your spouse can, work at making the emotional adjustment, no matter how hard you find it to be. That's because—and I want to emphasize this point I've made before because it's so important to your happiness—almost all retirement problems involve you and your spouse. Unless you're able to get along together, you won't be able to get along with the world.

The fourth pivotal emotional event is the loss of family unity.

YOUR REACTION

1. Stay close to your children by being a self-sacrificing grandparent.
2. Realize that your children are grown and that they should stand on their own feet, and help out only in emergencies.
3. Restore the three-part family unit (grandchildren, children, grandparents) by becoming a liberated grandparent.

EVALUATION OF YOUR CHOICE

Reaction 1 is an emotionally immature reaction; 2, a good emotionally mature reaction; 3, a triumphant emotionally mature reaction.

The fifth pivotal emotional event is the loss of the respect of your community.

YOUR REACTION

1. Acknowledge that as you get older, you become a member of a minority group (senior citizens), and accept your role passively.
2. Fight against discrimination by yourself and through organized groups.
3. Live up to your community's standards of acceptance and become an accepted citizen, not a second-class senior citizen.

EVALUATION OF YOUR CHOICE

Reaction 1 is an emotionally immature reaction; 2, a good emotionally mature reaction; 3, a triumphant emotionally mature reaction.

The sixth pivotal emotional event is the loss of looking middle-aged.

YOUR REACTION

1. Admit you're older, say "What's the use?" and let yourself run down.
2. Fight to keep that middle-aged look through fashion, exercise, cosmetics—even plastic surgery, if you choose.
3. Recognize that you can be attractive when you take care of yourself, groom yourself to suit your face and body, and keep active at things you want to do.

EVALUATION OF YOUR CHOICE

Reaction 1 means an emotionally immature reaction; 2, a good emotionally mature reaction; 3, a triumphant emotionally mature reaction.

The seventh pivotal emotional event is the loss of your spouse.

YOUR REACTION

1. Feel that your life is ended (because your life was so dependent on your spouse's) and live as a semi-recluse.

2. Go man- or woman-hunting as soon as your grief lets up.

3. Lead a full life after your period of mourning because you've prepared for it by living alone together, and fight off loneliness with the new friends you make by satisfying the emotional needs of others. (Remember, one of those friends could become your new spouse.)

EVALUATION OF YOUR CHOICE

Reaction 1 means an emotionally immature reaction; 2, a good emotionally mature reaction; 3, a triumphant emotionally mature reaction.

If you chose every reaction 3, you can predict that in retirement, you'll

- work
- earn enough money to offset the ravages of inflation
- have a happy marriage

- be closer to your children and grandchildren than even before
- become a first-class citizen of your community
- look attractive
- have a full life, even after the death of your spouse

You'll have turned seven of the most severe losses anyone can suffer into triumphs.

Doesn't your triumph over those losses bring new responsibilities?

Yes. You have a responsibility to work and earn money. You have responsibilities to your spouse, to your children and grandchildren, to yourself, to your friends, and to your community.

They replace the middle-aged responsibilities you shed.

But there's an enormous difference between the two kinds of responsibilities. The responsibilities of middle age were thrust on you. The responsibilities of retirement are accepted freely because you know that life without responsibilities is barren and futile. Your emotionally mature retirement attitude is: I must take on responsibilities to make my life worthwhile.

You can take on retirement responsibilties mainly to yourself and get ample emotional satisfaction.

Or, you can take on retirement responsibilities to yourself and to others and get the highest degree of emotional satisfaction.

The first choice can give you a good life; the second can give you a triumphant one.

In your new world of retirement, filled with responsibilities to others as well as to yourself, will there be any room for the development of the real you?

Make your own prediction.

The eighth and final pivotal emotional event is the loss of your middle-aged way of life.

YOUR REACTION

1. Continue to play the same roles in retirement that you did in middle age and wonder why you're miserable.

2. Get rid of your middle-aged responsibilities and work at play, or at learning, or at doing nothing.

3. Drop the roles you played in middle age and uncover the real you; then go on to realize your true potentials.

Your triumphant emotionally mature reaction is 3.

But since you've accepted new responsibilities to yourself and to others in retirement, you adopt this new emotionally mature retirement attitude: I must use my retirement responsibilities to myself and others to realize my true potentials.

Here's an example of that attitude at work for you.

The real you, you discover, has these potentials: the gift of making people happy, the ability to create miracles in the kitchen, and the capacity to enjoy a modestly comfortable life.

This is the way you use your new responsibilities to realize your potentials.

- You have responsibilities to many people, from your grandchildren to people in your community whom you've never met. Make them happy. You can do it when you read their emotional needs and satisfy those needs (see chapter 10). Your efforts are likely to carry you into doing volunteer work for hospitals and charities, cheering up the ill and impoverished. You do it in some of the time you have away from your real work. It's a fine thing to do; volunteer work here is not a work substitute but an expression of the real you. You can see the gratitude and the affection in the eyes of those you comfort. Your potential to make people happy is fully realized—you help people, and you lead a richer emotional life.

- You learn more about the art of cooking. You take classes in your spare time; you bone up on haute cuisine in your local library. You practice and perfect your skills. But you don't just pile up knowledge for knowledge's sake. You know you have a responsibility to others. You invite friends and relatives to your sumptuous repasts and bask in their admiration. You teach and open a catering service from your home or even a small restaurant—and earn money, too. Your potential to work miracles in the kitchen is fully realized—you turn your dishes into praise, excitement, and profits.

- When you accept all your retirement responsibilities to yourself and to others, you earn as much money, love, friendship, and emotional support from your community as you need. Your potential to live a modestly comfortable life is realized to the limit of your capacity.

When you've reached a high degree of emotional maturity in retirement, you make the triumphant decisions that bring you new responsibilities to yourself and others. It is by making use of these responsibilities that you're able to become the real you that you have always wanted to be, to fully realize your potentials. And when you realize your potentials, as you've just seen, you live your life to the fullest. Your triumph of age is now complete.

What is the triumph of age?

When you're emotionally mature for retirement, you feel happy because you've solved your retirement problems, and you feel vital because the solution of your retirement problems relieves you of the stresses of aging. And when you reach a high degree of emotional maturity for retirement, you live your life to the fullest.

Feeling happy and vital while living your life to the fullest—that's the triumph of age.

One final prediction.

The triumph of age is in your future.

Suggested Readings

A number of books on aging and retirement problems are available that can help you come to grips with life after retirement. This is my selection of those books based on the authors' ability to make their points in a no-frills fashion.

Adler, Joan. *The Retirement Book: A Complete Early-Planning Guide to Finances, New Activities, and Where to Live.* New York: William Morrow & Co., 1975.

Barbara, Dr. Domenick A. *Loving and Making Love.* Rockville Centre, N.Y.: Farnsworth Publishing Co., 1975.

Bellak, Leopold. *The Best Years of Your Life.* New York: Atheneum Publishers, 1975.

Bromley, D. B. *Psychology of Human Ageing.* Rev. ed. New York: Penguin Books, 1974.

Brown, Dr. Norman O. *Life Against Death: The Psychoanalytic Meaning of History.* Middletown, Conn.: Wesleyan University Press, 1959.

Butler, Robert N., and Lewis, Myrna I. *Sex After Sixty: A Guide for Men and Women for Their Later Years.* New York: Harper and Row, Publishers, 1976.

Carlson, Avis D. *In the Fullness of Time: The Pleasures and Inconveniences of Growing Old.* Chicago: Henry Regnery Co., 1977.

Coleman, Dr. Vernon. *Everything You Wanted to Know About Ageing.* London: Gordon & Cremonesi, 1976.

Comfort, Alexander. *A Good Age.* New York: Crown Publishers, 1976.

De Beauvoir, Simone. *The Coming of Age: The Study of the Aging Process.* New York: G. P. Putnam's Sons, 1972.

De Ropp, Robert S. *Man Against Aging.* New York: Grove Press, 1962.

Dickinson, Peter A. *The Complete Retirement Planning Book: Your Guide to Happiness, Health, and Financial Security.* New York: E. P. Dutton & Co., 1976.

Galton, Lawrence. *Don't Give Up on an Aging Parent.* New York: Crown Publishers, 1975.

Gass, William. *On Being Blue.* Boston: The Godine Press, 1976.

Gore, Irene. *Add Years to Your Life and Life to Your Years.* Briarcliff Manor, N.Y.: Stein & Day Publishers, 1975.

Griffith, W. D. *Hooray for Retirement.* Norwalk, Conn.: The C. R. Gibson Co., 1976.

Hess, Beth B., ed. *Growing Old in America.* New Brunswick, N. J.: Transaction Books, 1976.

Hoyt, Murray. *Creative Retirement: Planning the Best Years Yet.* Charlotte, Vt.: Garden Way Publishing Co., 1974.

Knopf, Olga. *Successful Aging.* Boston: G. K. Hall & Co., 1977.

Kübler-Ross, Dr. Elisabeth. *On Death and Dying.* New York: Macmillan, 1969.

Leaf, Alexander, and Launois, John. *Youth in Old Age.* New York: McGraw-Hill Book Co., 1975.

Lockerbie, Jeanette. *Fifty Plus.* Old Tappan, N. J.: Fleming H. Revell Co., 1976.

Lynch, Dr. James J. *The Broken Heart: The Medical Consequences of Loneliness.* New York: Basic Books, 1976.

Masters, William H., and Johnson, Virginia E. *Human Sexual Inadequacy.* Boston: Little, Brown & Co., 1970.

McGrady, Patrick M., Jr. *The Youth Doctors.* New York: Coward, McCann & Geoghegan, 1968.

Moody, Dr. Raymond A., Jr. *Life After Life.* New York: Bantam Books, 1976.

Retirement Living Magazine. *Your Health and Your Home in Retirement.* New York: Grosset & Dunlap, 1977.

Rosefsky, Robert. *Rosefsky's Guide to Financial Security for the Mature Family.* Chicago: Follett Publishing Co., 1977.

Ross, Jennie-Keith. *Old People, New Lives: Community Creation in a Retirement Residence.* Chicago: University of Chicago Press, 1977.

Schmidt, K. O. *The Beauty of Modern Maturity.* Translated by Leone Muller. Lakemont, Ga.: CSA Press, 1977.

Schuckman, Terry. *Aging Is Not for Sissies.* Philadelphia: The Westminster Press, 1975.

Schwed, Peter. *Hanging in There! How to Resist Retirement from Life and Avoid Being Put Out to Pasture.* Boston: Houghton Mifflin Co., 1977.

Sheppard, Harold L., and Rix, Sara E. *The Graying of Working America: The Coming Crisis in Retirement-Age Policy.* New York: The Free Press, 1977.

Sunshine, John. *How to Enjoy Your Retirement.* New York: Amacom, 1975.

Tanner, Ira. *Loneliness: The Fear of Love.* New York: Perennial Library, 1973.

Turk, Ruth. *You're Getting Older, So What?* Scottdale, Penn.: Herald House, 1977.

Weiss, Dr. Robert S., ed. *Loneliness.* Cambridge, Mass.: The M.I.T. Press, 1974.